Gwathmey Siegel Houses

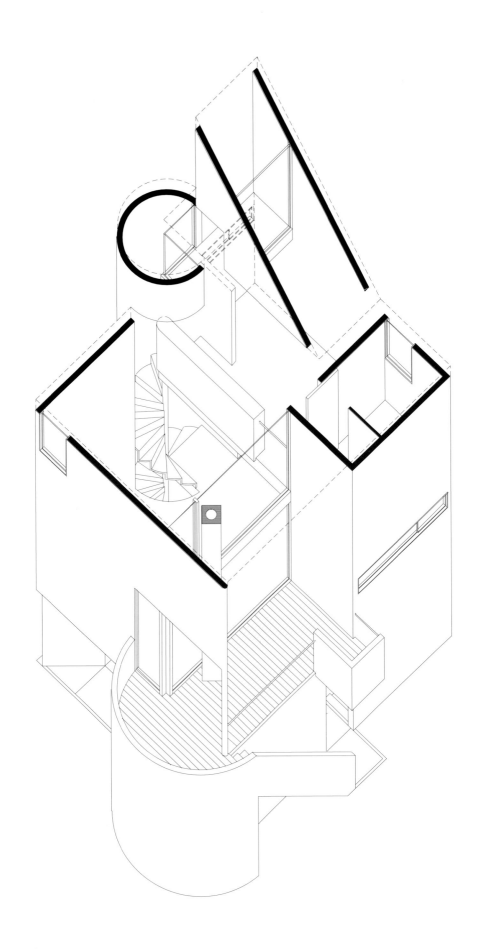

Gwathmey Siegel Houses

Foreword
Robert Siegel

Preface
Robert A.M. Stern

Introduction
Paul Goldberger

Edited by
Brad Collins

THE MONACELLI PRESS

First published in the United States of America in 2000 by
The Monacelli Press, Inc.,
10 East 92nd Street, New York, New York 10128.

Library of Congress Cataloging-in-Publication Data

Gwathmey Siegel houses / foreword by Robert Siegel ; preface by Robert A. M. Stern ;
introduction by Paul Goldberger.
p. cm.
ISBN 1-58093-015-8
1. Gwathmey Siegel & Associates Architects. 2. Architect-designed houses—
United States. 3. Architecture, Domestic—United States. 4. Architecture, Modern—
20th century—United States.

NA7239.G83 A4 1999
728'.372'097309045—dc21
                                                    99-046640

Designed and composed by group c inc (BC, MM, CW, EZ)

Printed and bound in Italy.

Contents

Foreword

Charles and I have collaborated for thirty years, often sharing a desk, sitting face to face drawing and discussing ideas. We have completed three hundred projects, ranging in scale from a birdhouse to a university, but more than any other building type, it has been the exploration of the single-family residence that has set the foundation for and substantially shaped many of the architectural principles around which the work of our firm revolves.

Prior to the formation of our partnership, in 1965, Charles designed a house for his parents in Amagansett, New York. The house was unique in its time and remains so today. Its plan size is a little larger than a two-car garage, but you can walk through it without going in it. Plan, section, and elevation were developed on regulating grids having to do with human functions and dimensions. It is about volume, intersection, density, and the enduring characteristics of carefully chosen materials. It is about clarity and economy of means. Moving through and around the house is an inspirational and reassuring experience which reconfirms the importance of exploration and discovery.

This book is mostly about the unique vision, work ethic, and devotion of my partner. His commitment to the design of each residence has been total.

Preface

Introduction to the Davenport Lecture delivered by Charles Gwathmey on April 12, 1999, at the Yale University School of Architecture.

Together with his partner, Robert Siegel, Charles Gwathmey has been the author of a uniquely identifiable body of work that carries the ideals of modern architecture into the new century. Charles Gwathmey and I were students at Yale together. Now as then, Charles embodies a ferocious integrity in both his work and his personal behavior. Integrity, talent, and a continuing commitment to a clearly articulated set of aesthetic principles are his hallmark as an architect. Charles's student work was notable for its rigor, for its clarity, and for its high style. So is his work today. He has not changed, nor has the quality of the work, which, if possible, only gets better and better.

While most architects stumble along on a professional path, Charles has followed a clear line of development. One summer when Charles was a student—I think he had just completed his second year—he renovated a barn on Long Island, lifting it from vernacular roots to the lyricism of high art. The New York Times Magazine immediately snapped it up for publication. That was the beginning of an extraordinary and extraordinarily consistent career. While some Yale students of those days moved to Vermont and forged a highly intuitive, ad hoc, even deliberately chaotic approach, Charles Gwathmey went to New York, where he joined the office of Edward Larrabee Barnes, then one of the most sympathetic places to be for a young architect who wanted to share in a practice that was challenging and principled. Ed Barnes was Yale's master plan architect in those days, and his modest houses and small buildings at St. Paul's School and Haystack Mountain School were amazing, combining rigorous geometry with natural materials in ways never before accomplished within the framework of modernism. Charles Gwathmey contributed to Barnes's work as did other Yale graduates, including Giovanni Pasanella and Jaquelin Robertson.

Charles left Barnes's office to build a house and studio for his parents in Amagansett on Long Island. The rest is, as they say, history. Charles not only designed the house, he also participated in its construction. But this was no ad hoc do-it-yourself effort. The Rosalie and Robert Gwathmey house and studio were meticulously crafted to the smallest detail. Moreover, they were dazzlingly composed in relationship to each other and their site, with form and space entirely liberated from the constraints of the prevailing modernism to incorporate lost lessons from the cubistic architecture of the 1920s. Beginning his career with a landmark, Charles has not rested on his laurels. He has gone on to success upon success. And though his work is strongly individual, it is always sympathetic to its site and to its architectural context. For this reason, Charles's addition to Frank Lloyd Wright's Guggenheim Museum in New York, surely one of the most challenging commissions, is a model for its modest deference, a perfect example of that kind of distinguished "background" building that Paul Rudolph urged upon us thirty years ago. So, it is my pleasure to introduce the work of Charles Gwathmey, an architect who has reshaped the visual landscape of our time, and who has, when appropriate, shown us how one can gracefully defer one's own bold vision to that of others.

Introduction

It is sometimes difficult to be sure whether Charles Gwathmey and Robert Siegel strive for complexity amid simplicity, or for simplicity amid complexity. Their architecture is never plain, and it often seems to possess a degree of elaboration that, the architects' deep commitment to modernism notwithstanding, could almost be called baroque. And yet it is driven at all times by a search for clarity—a desire to make the presence of space evident, a desire to articulate form, a wish to reveal rather than hide.

It was right to have called Gwathmey and Siegel formalists in the early years of their practice, and for all the evolution that has occurred in their work, they are formalists today. The experience of architectural form and space is what moves them. The way shapes play off against other shapes, the way we perceive volumes when we pass through them—these are the things that preoccupy these architects, the things that incite their passions.

Their value system is an aesthetic one; they have not sought to reform the nature of society or even to offer ironic comment on it. Much, though emphatically not all, of their practice has long been devoted to the design of large houses, and as newly created wealth has become more substantial in this country in recent years—and as Gwathmey and Siegel themselves have become more senior in their profession—they have taken on a role not unlike that of the one played by, say, Delano & Aldrich or McKim, Mead & White earlier in this century, when those firms provided the rich with distinguished Georgian mansions. Gwathmey Siegel's work bears no stylistic resemblance to these, of course, and the comparison is abhorrent to those who cling to modernism's early utopian dogmas. But in an age in which modernism is no longer a radical style but an accepted one, and unquestionably now has come to possess a more vigorous formal than social agenda, the similarity between Gwathmey Siegel and the most eminent practicioners of residential design in the first decades of the century is undeniable. By the 1980s, when the firm was working actively for such clients as David Geffen, Steven Spielberg, Charles Koppelman, Ronald Lauder, and Ron Meyer, it was clear that it had established a position as perhaps the most distinguished blue-chip architectural name capable of providing well-to-do clients with impeccable modernist work of the highest order.

These clients—and all others—have the chance to work with architects whose manner must be described as intense, and whose engagement as fervent. Their lives have been devoted to a quest for form, a quest they have chosen to play out in the realm of real commissions, not theoretical ones. There are few fanciful renderings in Charles Gwathmey's sketchbook, few imaginary projects: it is the actual that excites him, that instigates an exploration of the possible. He sees the world with the deep emotion of the artist, but his dreams are of solutions more than of new problems. It is an imagination that probes deep, even if it does not always range wide. The struggle to make architectural form is an earnest as well as a patient search, and there is no expectation that the search contains an end.

In their quest toward form, Gwathmey and Siegel edit: they cut, they reduce, they push to get to the essence. And at the same time they add: they embellish, they invent, they explore. It is a particular characteristic of these architects that their process is one that involves addition as well as subtraction. Refinement is their highest pursuit, and it is sought by making things both more direct and more ornate. Minimalist austerity is no more their stock-in-trade than eighteenth-century classicism. If they seek anything, it is to evolve a form of modernist expression that marries the sensual richness of traditional architecture with the discipline and self-restraint of modernism.

It is not easy to transcend what in the minds of most people (and most architects) is a contradiction—opulence and self-restraint. Never mind that striving toward a combination of richness and discipline is precisely what energizes much of the greatest architecture of the past; indeed, what better way to define the architecture of the Italian Renaissance? The same can be said of Mies van der Rohe in this century, an architect who, in his determination to make an architecture both rigorous and sensual, clearly serves as a kind of conceptual model for Gwathmey and Siegel, though they have never chosen to follow a literally Miesian path in the shaping of their forms.

For all the symbolic appeal held out by his blend of richness and restraint, it is not Mies who has affected Gwathmey and Siegel most profoundly. That role obviously belongs to Le Corbusier, whose great buildings from the 1920s find their way more literally into the firm's oeuvre than the work of any other architect, not only in terms of elevations and details, but also in terms of their attitudes toward space. To Gwathmey and Siegel, space is real and tangible. They want to shape space, to explore its geometric possibilities, to make us feel their crafting of space as powerfully as we feel the textures of the wood, glass, stone, and steel they use to define it. But to see Gwathmey Siegel's work literally in terms of Le Corbusier is to misread it entirely, for it has always been a response to a much broader call of modernism, a call that they have answered by embarking on what we might call a career-long series of modernist variations. The architecture of Gwathmey Siegel is, in part, a fugue on themes first explored by Le Corbusier and Walter Gropius and Charles Rennie Mackintosh and Frank Lloyd Wright.

Yet only in part, and less and less as time goes on. Like many architects of this century who have been influenced by classicism's discipline but have chosen a different formal path, Gwathmey and Siegel began their career searching for a series of Platonic ideals—perfect form, perfect space, perfect proportion, perfect texture. The search for Platonic perfection, as expressed through the (often futile) attempt to create ideal space and ideal building forms that possess the coherence of pure geometric objects, holds far less sway over these architects now, after thirty years of practice, than it did before. Their sense, early on, that the architect's mission was somehow to make an image of a perfect world, and thereby make life itself more perfect, seems to have given way to a willingness to craft an architecture that is less pure, less coherent, and more inclined to express the complexities and imperfections of the world. It is an extraordinary shift, all the more remarkable because it has come with no outward change in style: Gwathmey Siegel's work is as deeply connected to the visual traditions of twentieth-century modernism as ever. But these architects look at modernism now less as an answer than as a starting point, less as an all-inclusive, closed system than as a language in which they will compose their own messages, messages that have become far more conducive to the ambiguity of late-twentieth-century culture.

So is this then the modernist language as a means of sending a postmodernist message? Not quite. It is more that Gwathmey and Siegel have always been deeply concerned with the realities of building - with the tactile reality of materials, the physical reality of construction, the social reality of human use. They are builders, not theorists, a distinction that has been visible since the house Charles Gwathmey designed (with Richard Henderson, his former partner) for his parents in Amagansett in 1965, and which marks the beginning, at the astonishing age of twenty-seven, of his mature work. The point is that for Gwathmey, architecture has always been a tectonic pursuit. He is not interested in making buildings of wood that strive for the plastic appearance of stucco; he wants to express the wood-ness of wood, as much as Louis Kahn wanted to express the brick-ness of brick. Not for nothing did Gwathmey's house for his parents have natural cedar siding – inside and out ; he was never the purest "white" architect, even though he first came to national prominence in 1973, as one of the featured architects in the book Five Architects, the architects who became known in the parlance of the day as the "whites," connoting both their reliance on the white forms of Le Corbusier and their preference for pure solutions that both literally and figuratively eschewed shades of gray.

But Gwathmey's work was gray, at least physically, if not ideologically, because of his love of the tectonic. His belief in the realities of building, and in the presence of architecture as a real and tangible thing dependent on materiality, caused him to make buildings that were, in significant ways, different from those of his fellows among the New York Five. The differences were apparent as early as the 1970s, but no one was inclined to make too much of them then, least of all Gwathmey himself, who seemed in those years inclined to play down the tectonic aspects of his work and sought to portray it as more theory-driven than it truly was. He believed himself to have embarked on a kind of Platonic search, even though his work was moving in small stages, through the late 1970s and into the 1980s, steadily away from the creation of ideal geometric forms. There is a continual, if gradual, movement toward the sensual; an increasing comfort with using color, often subtle and unusual colors, rather than the primary colors of Le Cobusier, and a willingness to accommodate certain eccentricities of program and site.

This evolution has accelerated in the last few years. The work has become demonstrably different, even though it remains as committed as ever to modernism as a formal vocabulary. This is not the moment to discuss whether modernism ever possessed, in a coherent way, more than a unifying formal vocabulary; surely its ideology was never the ironclad orthodoxy that the early modernists wanted it to appear to be. However much Gwathmey may have shared certain aspects of modernism as an ideological pursuit at certain points in his career, he seems to have put them aside now, having isolated the purely formal aspects of modernism and directed them to his own, far more contemporary purposes.

Charles Gwathmey defines the evolution in the firm's work as a movement away from the creation of ideal geometric forms and toward collage, toward an increasing comfort with the notion of assemblage. He speaks of this both in terms of the method of creation—that is, the process by which his houses are designed as proceeding from an actual assemblage of parts, rather than by carving and sculpting a single form—and in terms of perception, of the way in which his recent completed buildings are meant to be seen as collages rather than single objects. He cites a further distinction between his newer work and the earlier work of his firm: the way in which it engages the land rather than sits like abstract objects upon it.

The Zumikon house, completed in 1994, does establish itself, far more than such well-known Gwathmey Siegel residences as the de Menil house of 1983, as different from what will always be the iconic Gwathmey house, the brilliant, tiny house and studio for his parents in Amagansett. (How fresh and full of controlled energy that Amagansett house looks, even now, though it is in fact older than many of the architects who work in Gwathmey's office.) The Zumikon house is a series of pavilions, made largely of concrete, with vaulted roofs of lead-coated stainless steel. While the vocabulary of materials and shapes at Zumikon is consistent from one section to the other, it is a notably different set of materials and shapes from those of the earlier residential works. And even the most casual look at the house makes clear that this is not a single object but a cluster of structures, tucked into a sloping hillside.

Of course the firm's residential work has progressed gradually toward more complex forms for several years: the Taft house, of 1977, is more intricate than residences such as Weitz and Haupt which preceded it by just a couple of years; the de Menil house is more intricate than Taft (particularly in the way in which internal space is essentially layered); the Opel house, of 1985, begins the process of breaking down the overall mass into an expression of several discrete masses. But in most of the houses of the 1980s, there is a desire to minimize the perception of the house as a series of discrete forms, a wish to play down its complexity in favor of a single visual image. The layered nature of the de Menil house is not emphasized on the exterior, for example, or even expressed overtly at all.

It is this process—the attempt to make even the most complicated forms appear to be simple, basic, and unified—that has been so dramatically reversed in the firm's recent work. The two most significant recent houses, the San Onofre residence in Southern California and the immense, sprawling Hilltop residence in Austin, are both composed of disparate sections joined together by structural and circulation links, and both strongly encourage our perception of them as being made up of parts. There are no false wholes here though; as in the case of the Zumikon house, the language of materials and shapes is so consistent within each house that the appearance of an assemblage of parts hardly implies an overt sense of disjuncture or fragmentation. The place appears all of a piece, though it is made up of many pieces. The houses are compositions of many parts as opposed to broken up remnants of a single, purer object. And once again, these newer buildings embrace the land rather than position themselves primly upon it—indeed, the San Onofre house, set at the top of Malibu Canyon, all but clings to the sharply sloping grade. In Austin, meanwhile, the land has been graded to build up a hill fourteen feet on one side to enhance the sense that the house has been set into the land, rather than placed bluntly on it as Gwathmey might have done a few years ago.

The expression of complexity at the San Onofre house, while earnest, is not, however, fully resolved. The mass of the house is divided vertically between a three-story curved limestone pavilion overlooking the Pacific Ocean, which is described as housing the main living spaces, and a three-story cube set into the canyon, which contains what Gwathmey describes as support spaces. In terms of the reality of its internal functioning, however, the house is divided horizontally more than vertically—there are some public spaces in both the limestone pavilion and the support cube, and some private spaces in both sections as well, making the split, in the end, appear to be dictated at least as much by purely formalist concerns as by organizational ones. This inconsistency between theoretical justification and actual experience does not deny the splendid, monumental sweep of the public rooms in the San Onofre house, or the striking visual drama of the break between the rusticated limestone section (its texture a striking reminder of Gwathmey's continued interest in exploring new visual possibilities) and the rest of the house. Indeed, it might more be taken as an object lesson in the dangers of excessive theorizing regarding an architecture that, even as it moves in new directions, continues to aspire to a fundamentally formalist aesthetic. To call the exterior of the San Onofre house a stunning composition more than an expression of theory is only to praise it.

At Austin, the vastness of the project—28,000 square feet—means that the organizational system has to be somewhat more rigorously connected to the experiential realities. Here, the great achievement is in the subtle balance between parts and wholes, and in the effort to use the topography and compositional elements of the architecture as a means of reducing the visual impact of a mass that is institutional rather than domestic in scale. The house does not deny its great size—to do so would be to embrace a coyness that is alien to Gwathmey's sensibility—though neither, happily, does it flaunt it. But here Gwathmey's increased interest in expression of complexity has been key to what is really the most important aspect of the Hilltop residence in the end: its quest to find within the modernist vocabulary a means of expressing domesticity on a monumental scale.

What is stunningly beautiful in a Gwathmey design, what takes your breath away, has always been the finesse of detail, more than the sweep of space or the pleasure of composition, and that has not changed. Yet all of the firm's work today seems more willing to indulge in a somewhat more intuitive degree of composition—elements like the section of the San Onofre house that cants outward as it rises, or the swooping roof of the natatorium in the Hilltop house, not to mention the bottle-like shape of the glass-enclosed breakfast room and master suite, all of which are splendid visually, are possible to justify only as purely compositional elements, not as expressions of theoretical intent. This is hardly to say that these houses or any of the recent projects are casually designed. Quite the opposite. But the precision and care that has gone into them has been directed as much toward pure visual appeal as to clarity of expression, and there is something less tight, less rigid, about the way they look when compared to the earlier projects. If the link between the two sections of the San Onofre house works well both compositionally and functionally as an entry, for example, then Gwathmey is willing to let it be one, despite the view he held for so long that letting a linking element serve also as an entrance blurs the distinction between various aspects of the composition.

Now, such ambiguities are accepted, even sought, as a way of enriching the work. It is a sign, surely, of maturity, as the architects move further away from the search for Platonic form with which their careers began, and come more to accept the notion that architecture can comfortably and reasonably express the ambiguity and contradictions of life. Gwathmey and Siegel have always acknowledged the reality of the physical conditions of architecture; indeed, their commitment to the tectonics of building has grounded their work since the beginning. And yet, for all that their reality base exceeds that of many of their peers, there has always been a certain innocence, too, in their work, born of the belief that the architect need only find perfect form and perfect details to fulfill his mission. Now, with another decade of work behind them, Gwathmey and Siegel have come implicitly to acknowledge that there is no promised land, at least not the Platonic one they first envisioned, and that while architecture may still strive for the purity of the heavens, it is possible for it to find its beauty by expressing the complexity and ambiguity of life on earth, and that such a quest may even be the nobler one.

Gwathmey Residence and Studio

When my mother and I bought the land in Amagansett, a one-acre flat field with views across the dunes to the ocean and surrounded by undeveloped land, my mother said, "Build me a house. I have $35,000. Do what you would do for yourself, just take our program and make believe it's yours." That, in fact, is the way we do all the houses. We inherit the program from the client, we take the site, we take the orientation, we take all the things that affect or impact the opportunity and we make it our own. In that way we become so integrated with and emotionally a part of the process that it could never be detached or automatic or repetitive. Each time it's an invention.

The chance to build this house for my parents was an incredible opportunity. Building it clarified for me that architecture doesn't have to be big to have presence or content; that a building, as an object on the land, though small, in this case only 1,200 square feet, can occupy a site with sculptural monumentality. This house, being small in plan, yet vertical, functions as both a piece of sculpture and a building that, at a different scale, could be read as a sculpture in a park. How it is placed and how it establishes its form is primary to its reading. This is an idea that can be traced back to Greek temples, objects that were clearly man-made, sitting on the land, not in the the land.

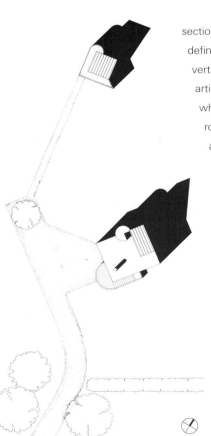

In this house, as in all our houses, it is the section rather than the plan that is the primary space definer. It is the volumetric manipulation and the vertical, rather than the horizontal, description that articulates and defines the space. The lower floor, which includes two guest rooms and a work room, is made private by the ceiling and floor above. The living level is open and is modulated by the insertion of the ceiling over the dining room, above which is the studio loft. The volumetric manipulation of the space is revealed through the intersection of forms, which is further enriched by the interplay of natural light.

Raising the "public" spaces—living, dining and kitchen—one level above grade capitalized on the views and established a relationship between the living space and the ground plane that was, at the time, unique to modern rural house architecture.

View from south over dunes

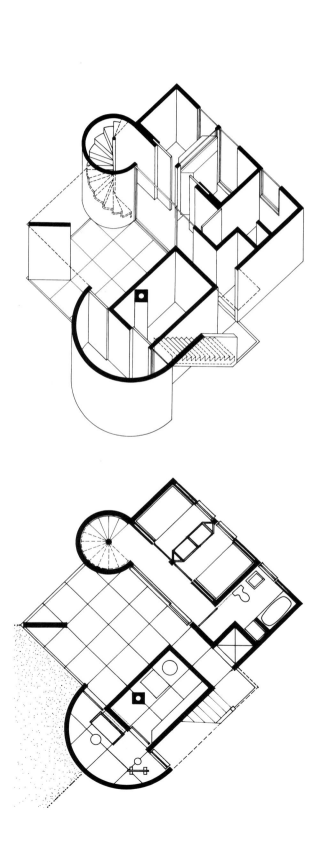
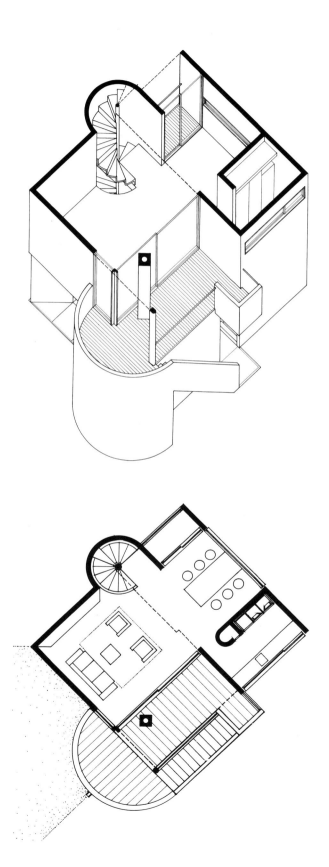

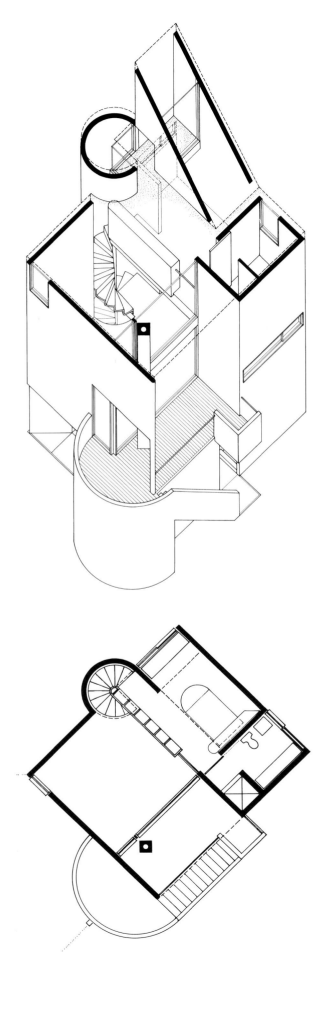

By placing the continuously occupied portion of the house above a base of intermittent functions, the "parlor" floor was reinterpreted and a sense of privacy established. This was an interesting reinterpretation since the traditional house always placed the public living spaces on the ground level and the private spaces above. Le Corbusier's Villa Savoye at Poissy and Stratford Hall, Robert E. Lee's grandfather's house in Virginia, have always been referential and precedents for me. Stratford Hall has two incredible outdoor stairs that bracket the parlor floor and access the lawn, which is treated as the base of the object. There are always historical references, but they are not literal, nor are they conscious—they are part of memory.

The house is composed of primary geometric forms that appear to be carved or eroded from a solid volume rather than constructed as an additive planar assemblage. The use of cedar siding on both the interior and exterior of the building furthers this reading and establishes a primary referential object. The use of the vertical siding, as opposed to shingle or clapboard, was an invention at the time and established a primary material palette, but it was not about the materiality. It was about abstraction and establishing the form as presence. The house is unadorned and undecorated. It relies totally on the solid-void compositional integration, rather than the traditional language of house architecture, the vernacular language that was prevalent in East Hampton at the time and has prevailed as the dominant "style."

Within a limited budget, a formal parti and vernacular were developed in this house that set a precedent for our later work.

Southeast facade

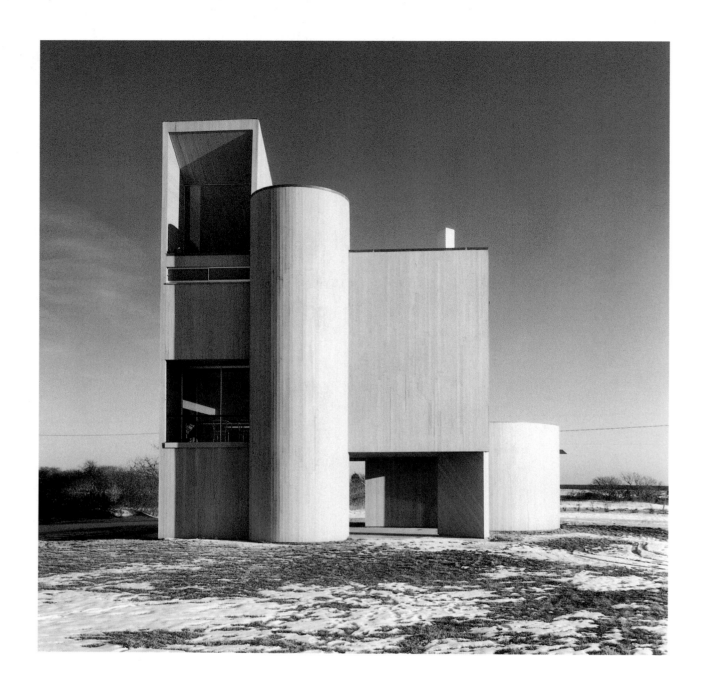

Northwest facade

View from west

Dining and balcony from living

View from studio/sleeping balcony

Detail of studio/sleeping balcony

Stair detail

Gwathmey Studio

A year after the house was built, I designed a separate studio building for my father. It contains, on the ground floor, a guest bedroom and, on the second floor, the studio with a large north-facing clerestory window and a very narrow, south-facing, horizontal slot window that allowed him to look back at the site and the house. Separating the studio from the main house allowed my father to walk outside and across the site; to leave where he lived and walk to where he worked was a psychological and physical enrichment to the lifestyle of my parents.

The plan geometry of the building is an eroded square. The bedroom is a square, and the overall building figure is a square that has been cut away, revealing the triangular corner and the semicircular landing of the stair. In section, the peak of the roof reinforces the cube and is consistent with the main house in that it appears to have been carved from a solid.

The opportunity to come back to the site a year later and build a second building was both a discovery and a confirmation. The addition of the studio extended and enriched the site/object relationship. The studio's section is derived from the house, but by siting it at a 45-degree angle to the original structure, a perceptual dynamic of corner versus facade was created. As one reads the house frontally, the studio is read from the corner. Its "objectness" is immediately three-dimensional and contrapuntal. One never perceives one building in facade without seeing the other rotated. So there was a constant interplay and dynamic relationship between the two objects. As sculptural forms, they establish both their own presence as well as a dialogue in the landscape.

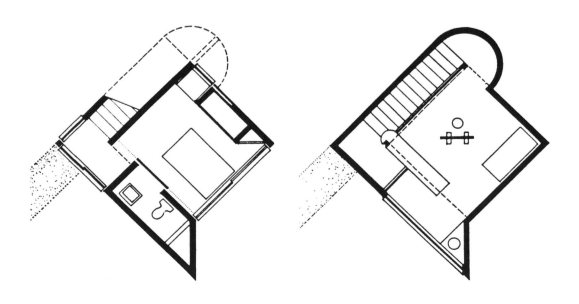

Ground and first level plans   *View north from drive to studio and house*

Studio and house from north

Straus Residence

This house for a young couple with two children sits in the middle of a large wooded site with no topographical variation. Local zoning ordinances required that a new structure enclose a minimum volume and be designed in the "colonial style" with pitched roofs. To enforce these precepts, there was a rigorous aesthetic evaluation of the proposed design by a town review board that was preoccupied with traditional and preconceived notions of what constituted acceptable architecture. These constraints provoked a reinterpretation of a known vernacular idiom.

The discovery and potential of designing a building with pitched roofs that would retain the volumetric integrity and extend the sense of spatial revelation that began with my parents' house was provocative. Though my parents' house reads as having a flat roof, there is an integrated diagonal form in the building: the shed roof over the master bedroom/studio. Here, instead of making one shed, we made two, each traversing the entire width of the building and containing a major clerestory window. These two forms are revealed in the interior from the entry hall, the stair, and the living room, becoming the defining elements of the space. They establish the silhouette of the house and articulate the volumetric clarity.

Unlike my parents' house, which sat on an open site, this house is discovered in a clearing at the termination of a long drive through the site. Rather than make a wood house, which, perhaps, would have been perceived as more integrated into the landscape, there was a conscious decision to create a counterpoint. The house's presence as an intervening white object on a plane, constructed of stucco rather than cedar, established a new sense of place. The house, through its transparency, becomes simultaneously a pavilion and an enclosure. It brings the woods in, but it is very much an environment. Like a tent sitting in a forest, it is an incredibly interactive shelter.

The house has a very simple "center stair hall" plan with the public spaces—living, dining, and kitchen—on the ground floor, and the two children's rooms and the master bedroom and dressing suite on the second floor. It is primary and, in the spirit of my parents' house, appears carved from a solid as opposed to being additive. It relies totally on its form and its volumetric integration to create its presence as an object, while being referential to a typical, traditional "center hall" plan.

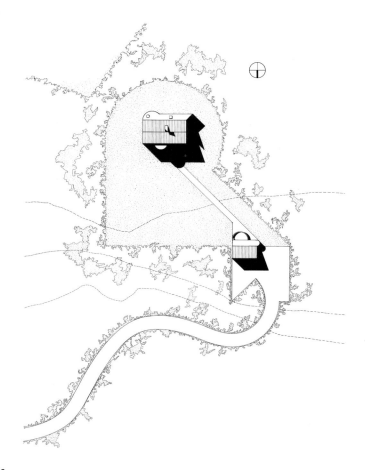

View from northeast

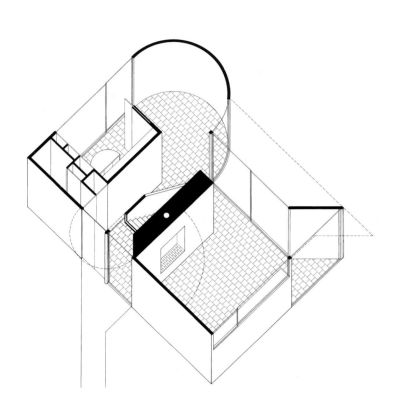

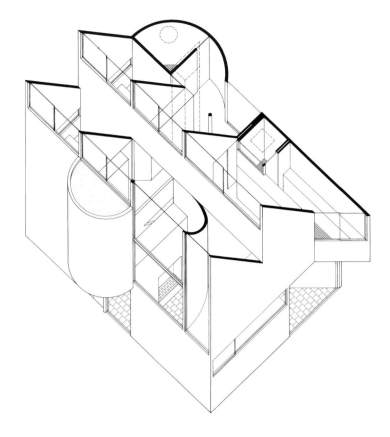

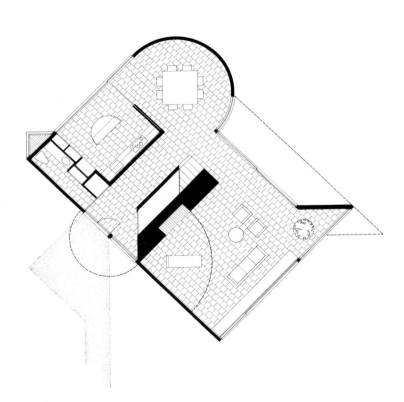

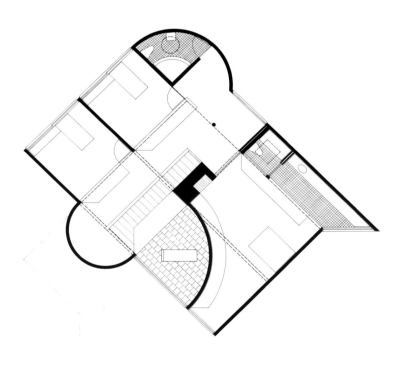

View from northwest

Sedecca Residence

Joe Sedacca was a graphic designer for the Museum of Natural History and loved modern architecture. He had purchased a fairly remote two-acre, sloping wooded site in East Hampton and wanted to build a very basic and simple vacation house. The parti, though programatically and organizationally different, was an extension of the technology and aesthetic of my parents' house. The program required a major living/dining space, a kitchen, a master bedroom/studio suite, a guest bedroom, and a storage structure that could eventually be converted to a second guest facility and garage. The design was derived from the constraints of a modest budget, a buildable site proximate to the road, and a desire for maximum privacy.

The storage structure defines the transition from the parking area to the entry walk, which leads directly toward the entry void in the curved volume of the front facade. The two-story living/dining space opens to an outdoor terrace, which engages the woods and is modulated by a sculptural chimney element that mediates the two-story glass facade. The space is airy and transparent, defined by the guest suite and kitchen on the ground level and the master bedroom/studio suite on the second level. The plan is geometrically elemental: a rectangle with a semicircular extension. The volume becomes more complex through the manipulation of the section and the juxtaposition of solid/void relationships. Of all of the early houses this was the most primary and least complex.

The commonality between the early houses is in the reduction of each into a basic and essential form that appears to have been carved away from a solid, the result of a geometric evolution and discovery process. Though each one has a different configuration, they are familial in that their readings are volumetrically and geometrically relatable. They are of their own character, not stylistically rooted in "house" architecture, each responding to site, view, orientation, public space versus private space, materiality, transparency, solid/void, and volumetric content. They are also each investigations of relatively small and not particularly complex programs, and each demonstrates a resolution that is specific yet shares a common strategy.

The materiality was also basic: formica cabinets, vinyl tile floors, electric heat, and cedar siding on the interior and exterior. The selection of materials in these first houses, which I built as well as designed, and how they were detailed, were thoroughly considered. Even though they look simple, craft and longevity were and always have been pertinent obligations of the work.

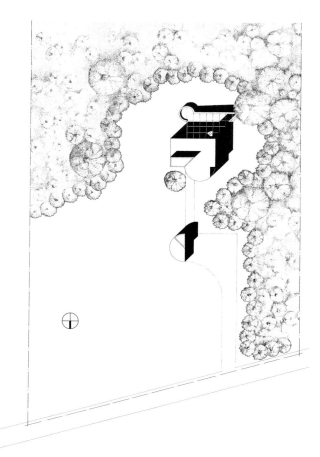

Storage building and north facade of house from drive

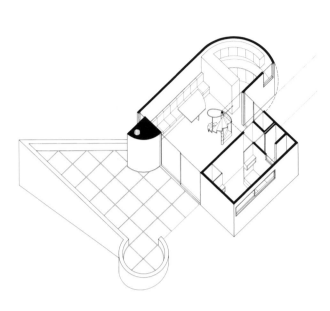

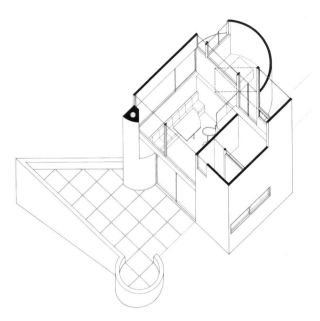

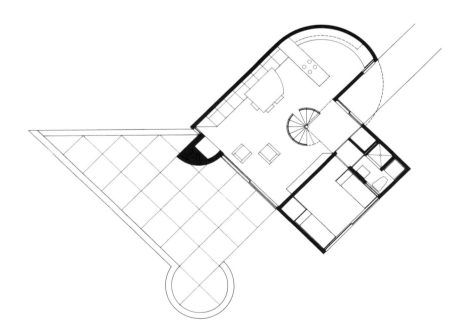

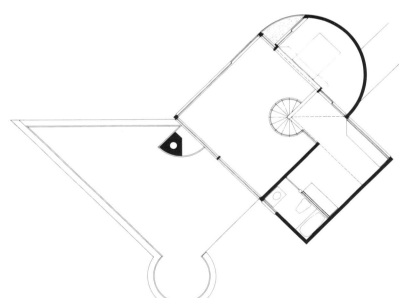

Living/dining from entry

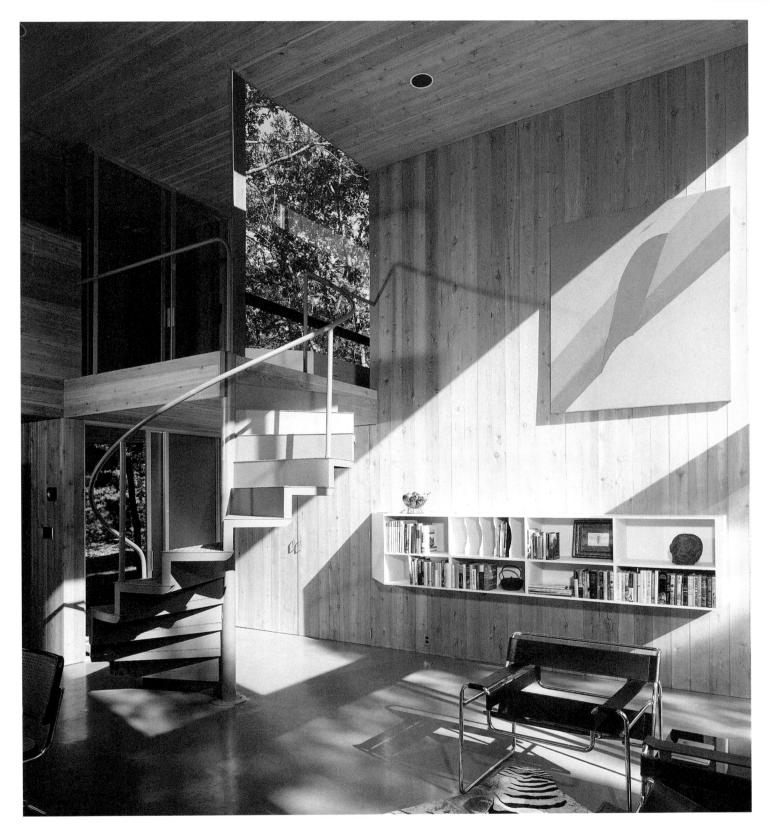

Balcony, living, and terrace from bedroom

Bedroom from studio

Studio from balcony   **59**

Living from balcony   *Detail of south facade and terrace*

Goldberg Residence

The clients, a builder and his wife, both wanted a significant modern house that was different from everything they had ever been in or seen. They were ideal clients. He had an understanding of how to build, was incredibly open to learning new systems, and became very involved in the whole making of the house. This was the first house I designed that another person built, where I was purely the architect. However, in this case, with the client being the builder, there was still a sense of integration between design and construction.

The house, on a wooded site with a steep slope, is both an object on a hill as well as being integrated into the contours of the land. In that way, this was a departure from the previous houses, which had all been objects on the land. As one approaches the house, it reads as a cornice to the site, revealing both a major primary solid, the semicircular library, and a major void, the one-and-a-half-story-high living space. Seeing this object in silhouette, especially at night, emphasized the dynamic of the solid/void relationship.

A grass terrace extends the living/dining area on the ground level literally and perceptually; it is an extension of the terrace idea developed in the Sedacca residence. The terrace becomes another room—spatially, as an extension of the interior, and formally, as an anchor to the hill. The terrace acts as a mediator between the landscape and the building, establishing "new ground" overviewing natural ground and defining the usable area within the extended site.

Southwest facade from drive

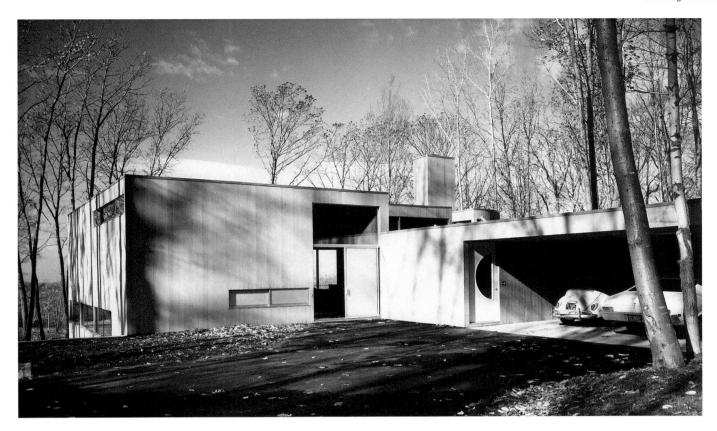

The parti was generated by the desire to have a basically horizontal organization with the children's rooms and the master bedroom in distinctly separate zones. The garage/storage, living/dining space, kitchen, and terrace were organized on the ground level, with the master bedroom suite and study one half level above, and the children's bedrooms and playroom one half level below. This organization not only separated the parents' bedrooms from the children's, it also separated the sleeping spaces from the main living space.

The split-level organization, a first for us, established the precedent where the children's rooms are detached from the parents' bedroom vertically, rather than horizontally as they would be in a traditional house. The children not only have their own rooms, designed with bunkbeds and desks under a window looking out to the woods; they have, in a sense, their own domain with direct access to/from the lower ground level. This vertical separation through the stair is legitimate architecturally and philosophically. As children grow up, the need for privacy, identity, and a space of their own supplants the need for proximity. The nature of life in a house is long term.

The materiality of this house was an extension of the other houses: cedar siding inside and out, slate floors, birch plywood and plastic laminate cabinet work, and aluminum framed sliding doors and windows. As the houses became larger and more complex, there was a second investigation of how to integrate the next layer of complexity into this first elemental and primary articulation. The strategies for that integration and that layering become an extended process of experimentation, revelation, and editing. Though bigger than the previous three houses, this house is still very simple and very elemental.

Stair to lower-level gallery and second-level study   *Detail of southwest facade*   *Living from terrace (overleaf)*

Cooper Residence

Built on a peninsula on the sound of Orleans, this house is a unique intervention into a conservative Cape Cod seaside village dominated by vernacular, Shingle Style architecture. The house established its presence as an object on the point and was accepted in much the same way that a lighthouse would be—as the odd object surrounded by water on an extended landscape.

The building site was limited to a knoll with access from the north. The house is very similar in organization to my parents' house, with the public spaces—living, dining, and kitchen—located on the parlor level, which vertically separates the private levels. Because of the sloping site, the entry is accessed by a ramp/bridge from the parking area and garage into the living or middle level of the building. The master bedroom is a balcony overviewing the double-height living space and terrace, and is extended by a semicircular deck above the dining space. The children's "dormitory," as the clients referred to it—three bedrooms adjacent to a playroom—opens to grade at the lower level. This access allowed the children, as in the Goldberg residence, to have their own domain.

In many ways, this is a transitional building, combining the siting strategies of the Goldberg residence and the three-story cube ethic of my parents' house: the composite plan/section overlay, the materiality and formal manipulation of transparency, and the volumetric interrelationships are all similar. It employs forms used in the first house, but is more elaborated. In retrospect, there was a preoccupation with using the semicircle as the primary counterpoint to the cube. In my parents' house the semicircle is used once; here it is used twice—once for the terrace off the living space, and again for the dining space and terrace off the master bedroom. As a pragmatic process of geometric discovery, this house represents the culmination of our early elemental formal strategy—the use of the 45-degree angle, the cylinder, the semicircle, and the cube—as well as its references to the primary geometric articulation of Kahn's plans and the volumetric organization of Le Corbusier's buildings.

The strategy in these houses, along with their distinct materiality, made them, as Vincent Scully said, "uniquely American." They were wood houses—not concrete or stone houses—and were an important extension of the Shingle Style. They were taut, their form articulated their volume, and there was no poché, no added thickness. The secondary and tertiary design elements were all in subsequent layers of accommodation—the materiality, the cabinet work, and the furniture—and were counterpoints to the primary forms and volumetric articulations.

This house—unlike the first three houses, which are clearly grounded, sitting either on the ground or in the ground—purposefully appears more precarious, as if it could walk into the water. And in that sense it is neither a lighthouse nor an anchor. The simultaneous tension between being in motion and being attached reinforces its dynamic relationship to the land and the water.

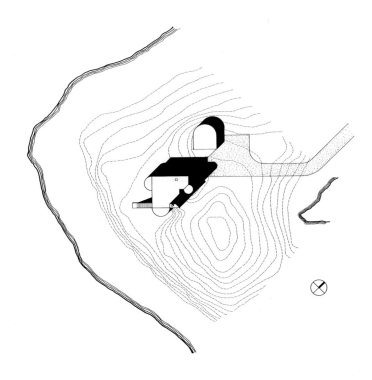

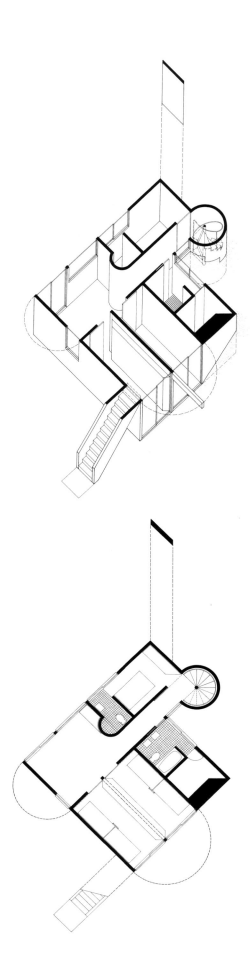
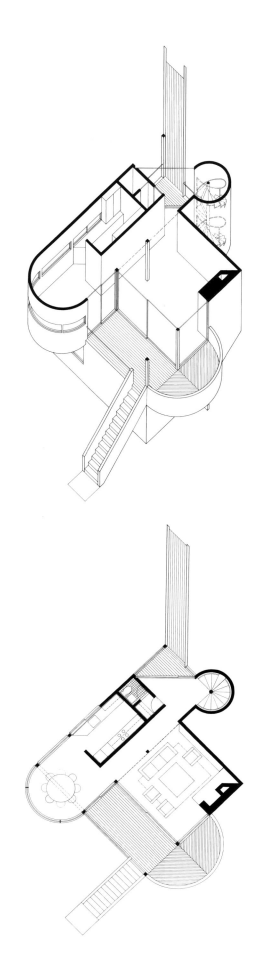

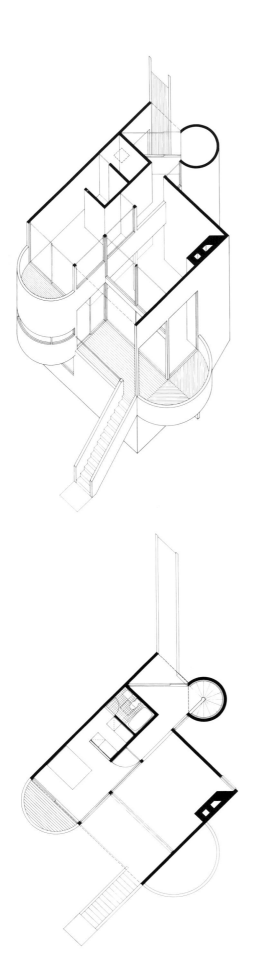

None of these houses are about elevation or facade per se, but rather they are about rotation and corner. This is an obvious observation in retrospect, but at the time it was more intuitive. The models and the organization of the space always generated the facades, as opposed to being developed as independent studies. This is critical in all of our work and gives our buildings their inherent three-dimensionality and "objectness."

Growth and opportunity come together at various points in the process, and when they coincide another level of experimentation is provoked. The best of the first discoveries are extended, and those that cannot be sustained are eliminated. It is never a totally conscious process of self-editing—it is more pragmatic than theoretical. The work has become more theoretical over time, but the theory has not been the driving determinate. Though I have become more articulate, self-critical, and philosophical over the years, I still believe that theory is analytical rather than generative.

76 View from south

Detail from deck to dining and master bedroom deck   *Master bedroom and deck*   *Dining*

View from north   *Northwest facade*   *Southwest facade*

Tolan Residence

It is unusual if not unique to persuade two separate clients with different programs on adjacent sites to agree to visually integrate the entire composition. But Michael Tolan was a friend of mine and, with my encouragement, bought the piece of land west of my parents' house. The program required a single living/dining/kitchen space, a master bedroom, three guest rooms, a game room, and a tennis court. The location of the tennis court was dictated by zoning regulations. Its size, a 60-by-120-foot rectangular plaque, was problematic relative to the scale of the house itself and to the two buildings on my parents' property. Treated in the traditional manner, isolated and surrounded by a chain link fence, the tennis court would have changed the overall scale and composition of the two adjacent sites. The solution was to integrate the tennis court into the house as a major space, creating a site

View from east (previous pages)   *Site plan; ground, second, and roof level plans and axonometrics*

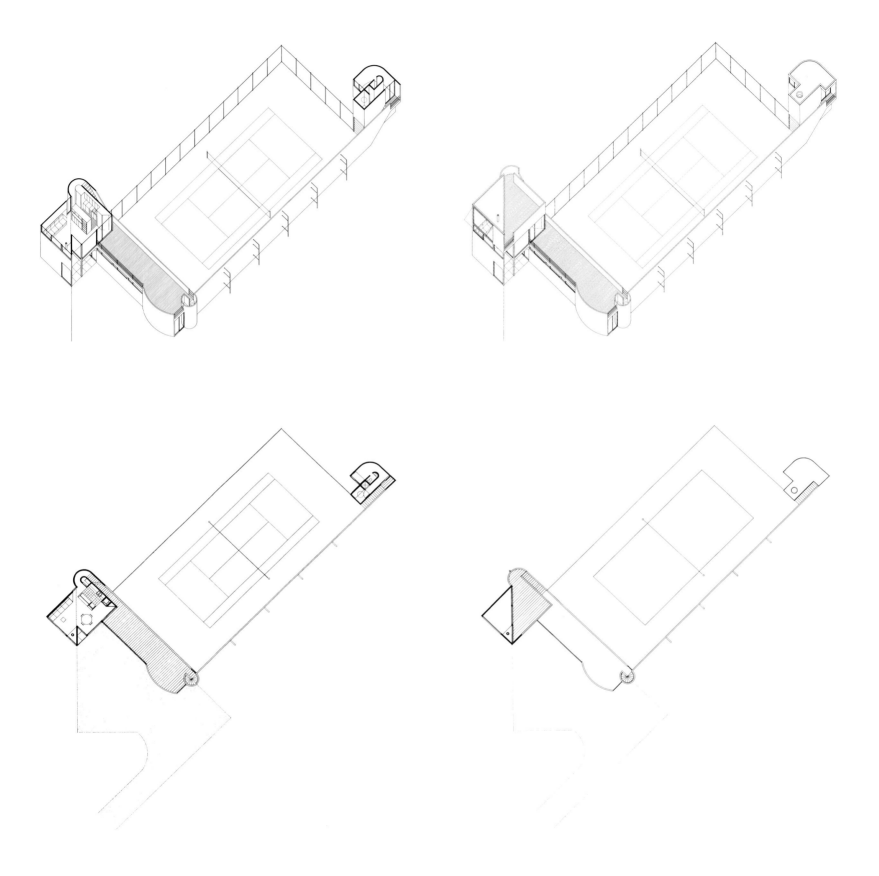

organization and building composition that simultaneously reinforced object identity while preserving programmatic intentions.

The east side of the tennis court, adjacent to my parent's property, is defined by a 12-foot-high, 120-foot-long, cedar-clad wall, articulated by steel pipe wind bracing. The "house" anchors the southern end of the tennis court. The master bedroom is located on the lower level, separated from the guest bedrooms by the entry, which also opens through to the tennis court. The living/dining/kitchen space occupies the second level and opens to a horizontal deck above the guest room/playroom area on the first level, and overviews the tennis court to the north and the ocean to the south. At the east end of the deck, a spiral outdoor stair reconnects down to the tennis court and the playroom. On the west end, another outdoor stair accesses a private deck above the dining/kitchen area with panoramic views of the ocean through the upper clerestory window of the living space. Raising the living level to the parlor floor was directly related to the parti of my parents' house.

Integrating the tennis court into the house resulted in a tripartite scheme, the precedent for which, though subliminal, was Pisa, where the basilica, cathedral, and tower sit on a grass plaque and are framed by the stone wall of the cemetery. The tennis court wall establishes the referential plane and counterpoint for my parents' house and studio; the master bedroom/living/dining/kitchen element of the Tolan residence becomes the volumetric anchor to the whole composition. The tennis court wall is the referential plane for the three objects, which present a sequence of oblique relationships to each other. The wall is a physical landscape mediator, providing both acoustic and visual separation, while allowing the two sites to interact as a single composition. My parents' house, successful in isolation, was made more dynamic by the addition of the studio. The addition of the Tolan house as frame and third element further enriched the architectural and site dialogue.

View from east   *View from upper roof deck*   *Living and dining with view to Gwathmey house*

Stair to ground level from kitchen   *Bedroom gallery*

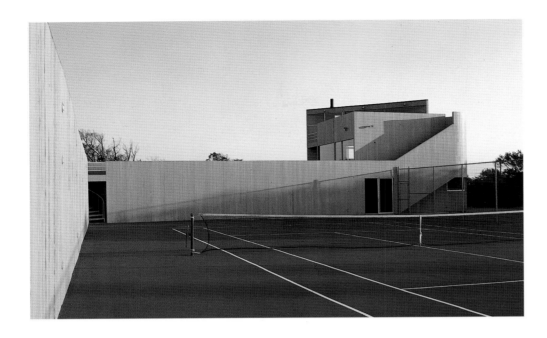

Northwest facade from tennis court

View from west

Cogan Residence

The Cogan residence was our third large house. The Steel Houses, built a year earlier, were extensions of the small house ethic. They were primary and singular—larger versions of the carved, eroded volumetric forms of the first series of houses. We learned that to simply expand the vocabulary and partis of those first small houses, to simply make them bigger, was problematic. Extending the strategy lost the essence, the compositeness and the tension. The resulting buildings were less dynamic and less consolidated. In the Cogan residence, for the first time, the "object building," with its articulated and small-scale representation, is combined with a large-scale referential pavilion structure. The object building is thus locked into the frame structure and extended horizontally and vertically through it. The counterpoint and juxtaposition between these two elements introduced an entirely different dynamic and level of enrichment to the work.

This strategy allowed us to create a building that responded simultaneously to the scale of the site—five acres with a pond on the south, and dunes and ocean beyond—as well as the scale of the program, which required a separate children's zone, incorporating three bedrooms and a playroom, a large living/dining space, a kitchen, a master bedroom suite with a sitting room and study, a separate guest suite, a staff bedroom, covered parking, outdoor storage, and a swimming pool.

The house is sited at the top of the gently sloping site to take advantage of the panoramic views. Again, the primary public spaces are elevated to the second level. The lower level accommodates the parking and service core (dumbwaiter and stair), the two-and-a-half-story entrance porch, the foyer, the children's bedrooms, and the playroom, which is half a level below grade. The lower level constitutes the base of the "pavilion," whose "roof" becomes the new datum for the major public space above. The pavilion is supported by a columnar structure that penetrates through the base building and simultaneously with the object building articulates the main volume.

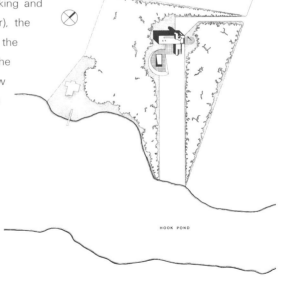

HOOK POND

SAND DUNES

ATLANTIC OCEAN

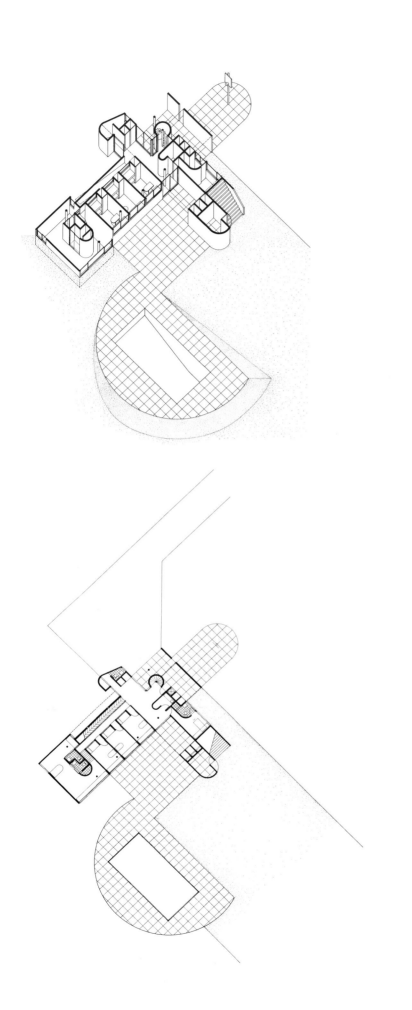
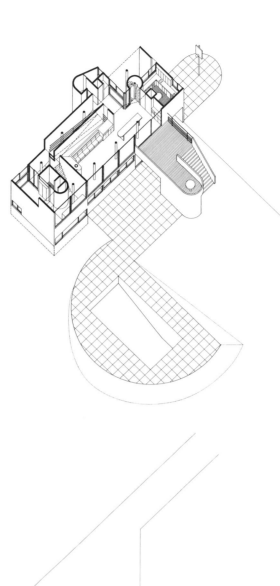
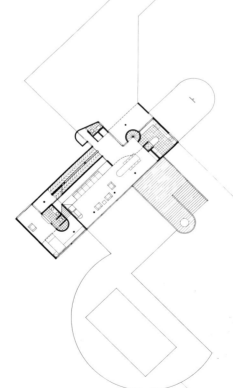

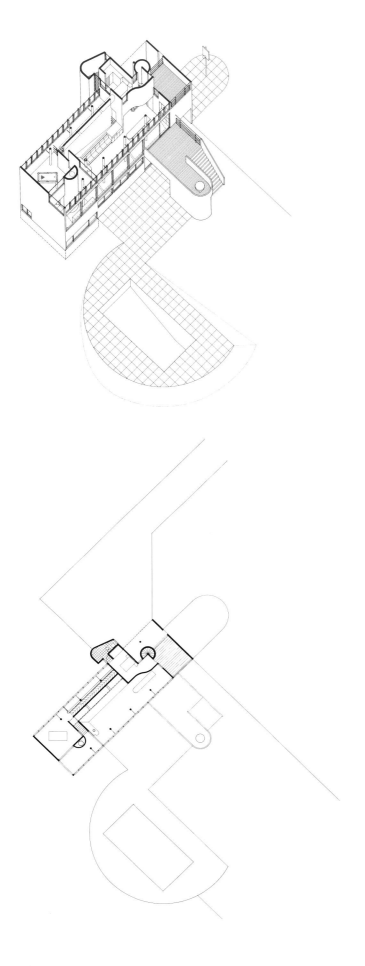

The lower level is zoned by the entry, which separates automobile and service areas from the children's area. The entry permits direct access to the pool terrace and changing rooms, and is the point of origin of a ramp, the primary circulation device for the house. The half-level landings and the linear circulation experience inherent in the ramp space develop multiple and sequential spatial and view experiences.

The first leg of the ramp parallels the children's bedrooms, which, with their doors and frosted glass interior clerestory windows, are articulated as outdoor entries. This sense of walking past the exterior of a building is heightened by the linear skylight two and a half stories over the children's corridor and by the use of the cedar siding inside and out. The first landing arrives at the master bedroom, a modulated one- and two-story space. The second landing, above the entry and looking down through the entry portico, is the one-and-a-half-story primary living space with a large deck and outdoor stair extension. The third landing arrives at the study, a balcony over the master bedroom, with its own internal stair reconnecting it to the bedroom below.

The guest suite is reached separately, by a spiral stair from the main entry level, and has its own roof deck with views of the site, the pond, and the ocean. These multiple vertical circulation strategies contribute to the sectional complexity of the house. The half-level displacements create an overlapping section as complex and interlocked as the interaction between the pavilion frame and the object building. These sectional devices reinforce the programatically required privacies—the master bedroom suite is separated from the children's zone and from the public spaces, while the guest suite is located at the top of the house as a roof element extending the "object building" vertically.

The Cogan residence represented a major extension in complexity and compositeness that became referential for our other work. On one level, all of the houses are formal studies, representing an ideal. They are ideograms of an interpretation of architecture. They are laboratories for developing strategies that are universal within our ability to investigate architecture. They are not idiosyncratic or stylistic, but paradigms. While we were designing the Cogan residence, we were simultaneously working on Whig Hall at Princeton. There we found the frame; in the Cogan residence we made the frame. The Cogan object building is familial to the Princeton intervention within the existing classic frame by virtue of their similar strategies. With the Cogan residence we discovered a new formal organizational strategy for the manipulation of scale and the articulation of separate elements that are not intended to be read as singular or consolidated, but rather as "collage" and contrapuntal.

Pool terrace from south

Ramp to second level

Living from dining

Living and dining from third level

Cohn Residence

The Cohn residence is the first of a series of four houses—including Haupt, Weitz, and Benenson—that extends and elaborates the strategies discovered in the Cogan residence. All are object-frame generated, of a similar size, and based on half-level or full-level site integration. All share the same basic programmatic organization in that the parlor floor becomes the public level, and each can be read as an architectural filter in the landscape—as a spatial and volumetric wall between the entry side and the view side of the site.

Unlike the Cogan residence, which is unencumbered by neighbors, this house is on an ocean dune site with a steep slope to the cul-de-sac access road and adjacent residences on the east, west, and north. Given the narrowness of the site and the proximity of other buildings, the urban row house, with its parallel enclosing side walls and open end walls, was a provocative precedent. In the Cogan residence, the frame is parallel to the site and view; here it is perpendicular. The side walls are more solid and less articulated than the front and back walls, which open to the views. This perpendicular orientation offers an opportunity for more complex layering and internal transparency—the sequential revelation of overlapping spaces that engage one another.

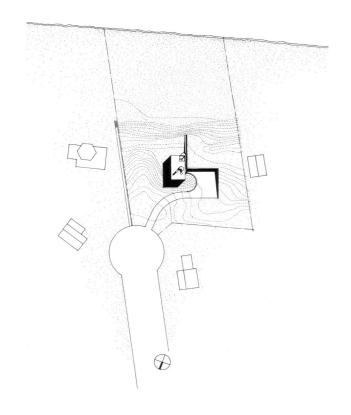

View from northwest

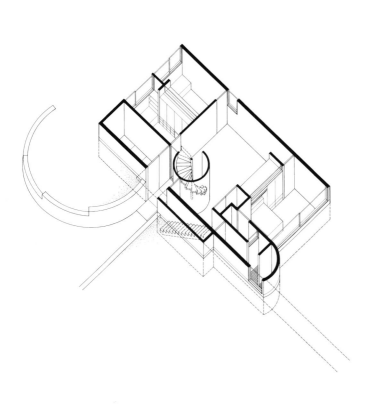

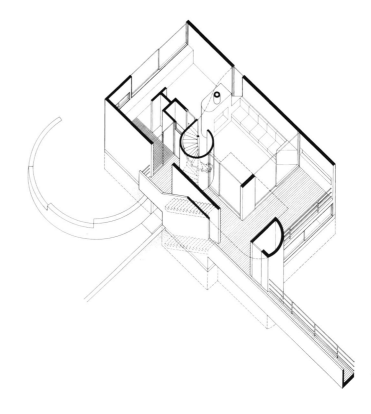

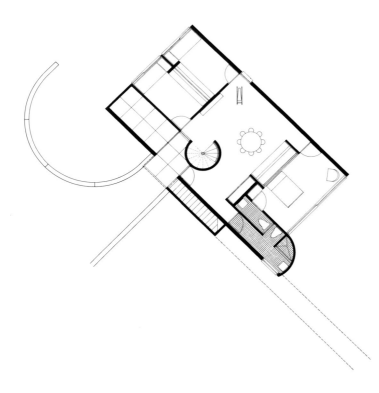

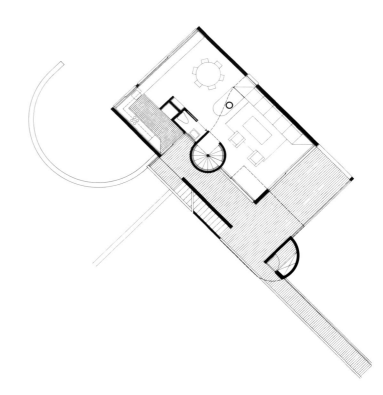

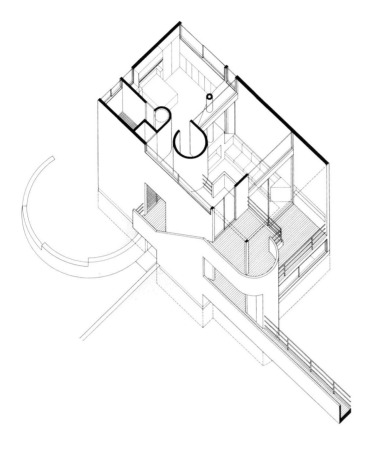

The program was distributed on three levels accessed by two overlaid but separate circulation systems. The exterior stair comes up from the auto court and connects the deck and the bridge to the beach on the second level as well as to the sun deck on the third level. This sequence integrates the building into the topography; like the Goldberg residence, it is a building both in the land and on the land.

The interior circulation system, a circular stair that is read as a cylindrical volume that both engages and extends past the frame, is accessed from the entry on the ground level, which also contains the two children's bedrooms, a playroom, and a guest bedroom. The second level accommodates the kitchen, with direct exterior access, dining, and double-height living space, which opens to a deck extension facing the ocean. The third level contains the master bedroom suite overviewing the living space and a balcony study with direct access to the deck, which terminates the outdoor circulation system.

The parti determined the vertical organization: the ground level established a base; the second level established a view orientation and provided access to the beach; and the third level established the private yet open adult spaces that were interlocked spatially and hierarchically with the second level. In hindsight, it is clear that the notions of internal transparency and layering that are most fully exploited and consolidated in the de Menil residence first incubated here.

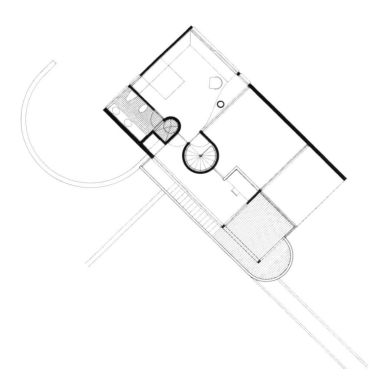

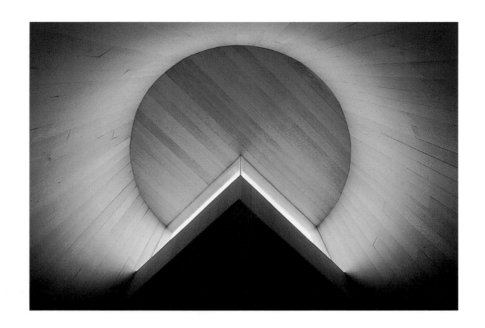

Detail at top of stair   *Detail of stair*   *Living*

Haupt Residence

The Haupt residence, on a one-acre site in the middle dunes, presented a new challenge—a house entirely surrounded by other buildings. To transform this condition we created an enclosed and private domain with views to the ocean across the other sites.

As in the Cogan residence, the frame in this house is parallel to the view and is organized in section, at half-level intervals, by a stepped ramp. The first two segments of the ramp, which parallels the entry facade, are articulated on the exterior and read as erosions in the primary frame. Zoning ordinances required that all living levels in a dune area be at least fourteen feet above sea level, thus placing the primary living spaces a half level above grade. The garage and entry are located on the north facade at grade. From the entry, the first leg of the ramp arrives at the living/dining, kitchen, and pool terrace level. Extending from the south facade, the pool terrace is oriented toward the view and light while functioning as an extension of the main living space. It is the referential outdoor space, creating a foreground for the horizon view.

The master bedroom suite has a private deck with an outdoor stair that connects to the pool terrace. This one-and-a-half-story volume over the garage and pool house is reached from the second ramp landing, one level above grade. The third ramp landing, a level and a half above grade, provides access to the study and the two guest bedrooms with their south-facing balconies above the pool terrace. The ramp and landings are articulated by a continuous skylight and overview the two-story living/dining space—the mediating volume that separates the master bedroom suite from the guest bedrooms in plan and section.

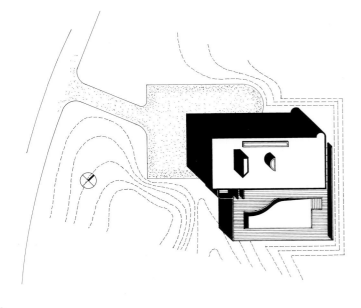

View from east

Ground/first and second/third level plans and axonometrics

The half-level sectional organization exploits the land configuration and creates the appropriate programmatic privacies. The house is a totally self-integrated indoor/outdoor building, but one that reads differently from the view and entry sides. From the entry or ground-related side, the building reads as a solid—clearly stabilized and anchored to the entry court. In contrast, the predominately glazed south facade is transparent and open to the pool terrace and view beyond, and reveals the internal layering and sectional manipulation. The continuous roof overhang completes the primary rectilinear frame and serves as a brise soleil for the recessed glazing. From the view side, the building reads as floating in the landscape. Divorcing itself from its context, it is a conscious intervention creating its own sense of place and "objectness."

The materiality of this house is different from all of our previous houses: for the first time we used a white stained cedar exterior with a painted gypsum board interior. By staining the cedar white, the different materials are integrated formally and visually. It was also the first time we introduced color as a coding element, adding another layer in the articulation of planes and intersections, and reinforcing the hierarchical relationships.

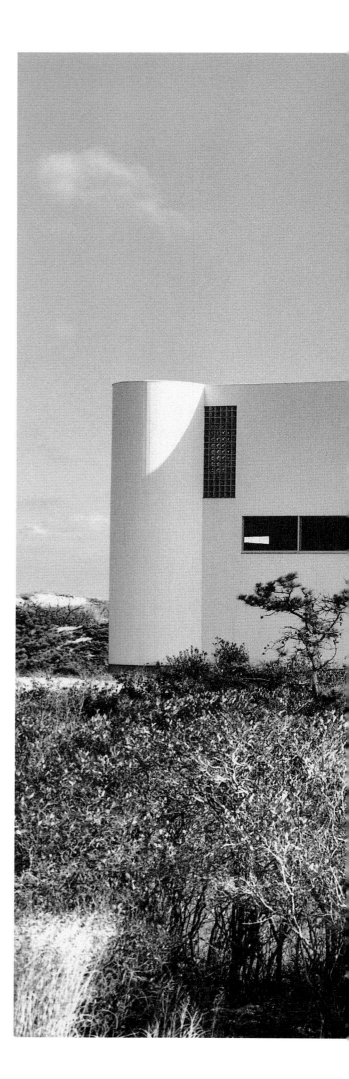

Ramp to first level from entry

Living

Ramp to second level

Pool terrace from master bedroom deck

Pool terrace

Weitz Residence

The Weitz residence, like the Cohn residence, is a "dune house" with adjacent structures to the east and west. Sectionally, the sites are very similar, as were the responses—one enters at grade level, the dune steps up, and the house, sited perpendicular to the view, is simultaneously a filter and a bridge between the entry side and the beach side. The idea of the house as filter translates into a sectionally manipulative and mediating wall between the two scales of water and landscape, unfolding and becoming more transparent as it extends vertically.

The house is a combination of the Cohn residence, in its "row house" parti and sectional organization, and the Tolan residence, in its integration of two masses anchored to an entry and a circulation core. Here, though, the integration is more complex in that it involves interior and exterior vertical and horizontal circulation systems, culminating in a bridge extension to the beach.

The program required a main house with a living/sitting area, dining, kitchen, a master bedroom suite, and two working studies. There was also a requirement for two distinct guest suites with kitchenettes and direct outside access, plus a carport, a swimming pool, a tennis court, and extensive outside deck space. Compositionally, the house is much more complex than the Cohn residence as the guest house/carport is a separately articulated though integrated element.

Because the house opened to two major views—the beach and the ocean on the south, and the bay on the north—the exterior program elements are used to establish a site strategy. The driveway, which is on axis with the carport, is parallel to and passes sequentially two "outdoor rooms": the tennis court and the pool terrace. The site and building layering are integral and sequential. By locating the pool on the bay side rather than the ocean side, the lower-level covered terrace and the adjacent pool area become a primary outdoor entertainment space, protected from the wind, as well as a viewing area adjacent to the tennis court.

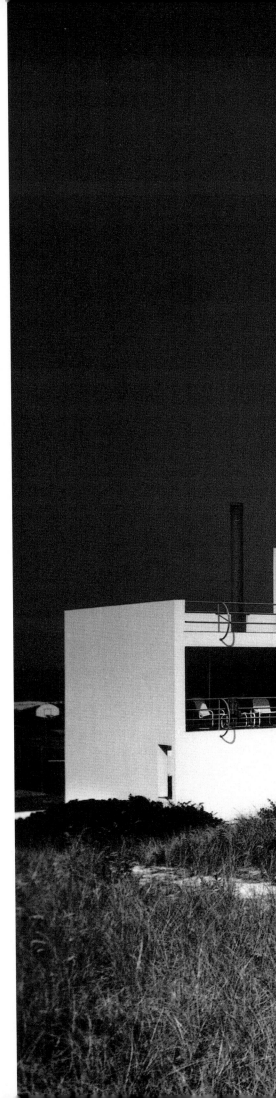

View from southwest

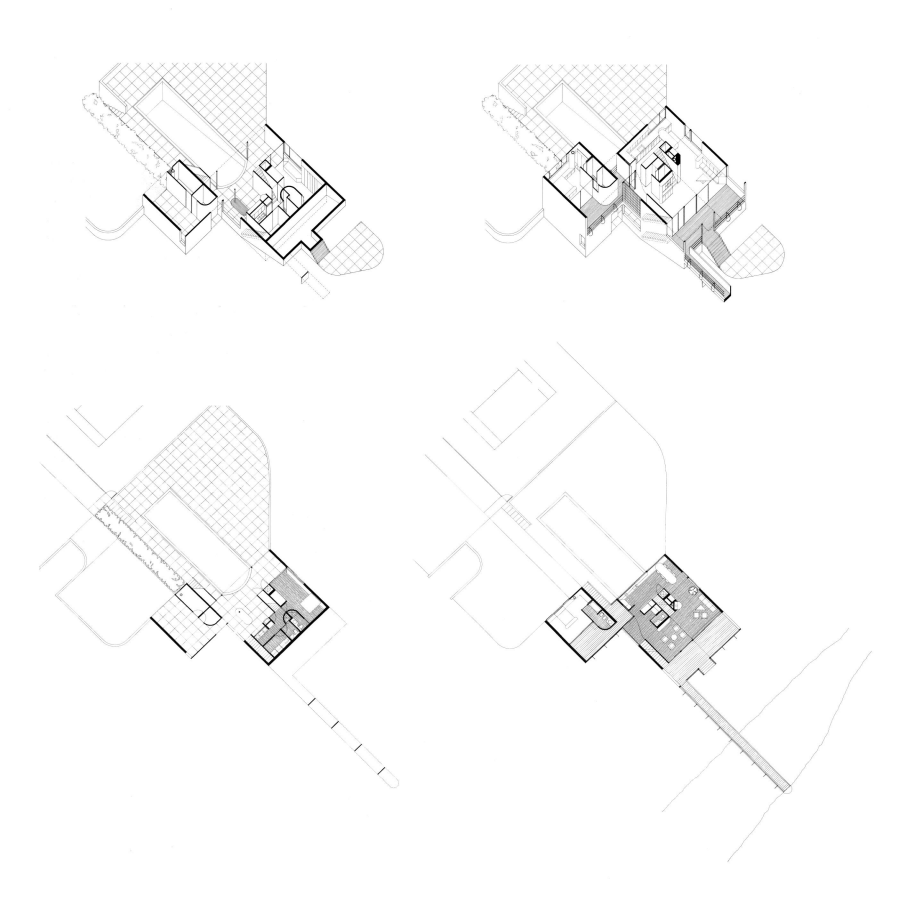

158   *Ground, first, and second level plans and axonometrics*

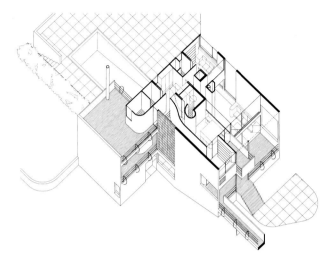

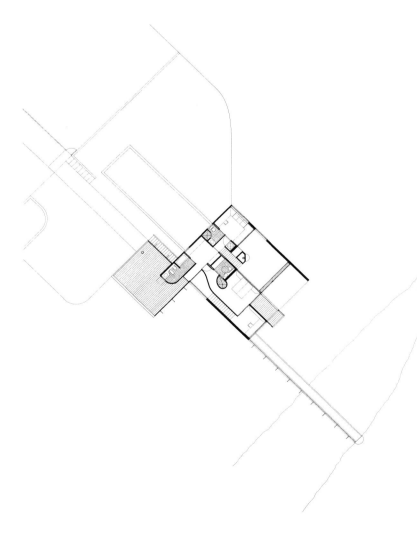

The entry stair is an integral extension of the ground-level pool terrace and connects the first-level outdoor deck space to the guest suite entry, the kitchen entry, the main entry and the bridge to the beach.

The first level of the main house is occupied by a single-height sitting area and adjacent double-height living space, both with access to the south-oriented deck with views to the ocean. The kitchen and dining area face north with views to the bay over the pool terrace and tennis court. The second level contains the master bedroom and a balcony overviewing the double-height main living space with extended views through to the ocean. Connected to the master bedroom are two separate studies—one at the top of the main stair facing the ocean, the other above the dining area at the top of the second stair—with views over the living space as well as to both the ocean and bay. An outdoor roof terrace over the guest house connects to the master bath/ dressing space and affords 360-degree views while maintaining its privacy.

The terrace mediates the interconnected series of outdoor spaces: the decks and the bridge, which face the ocean, the pool and the tennis court, which face the bay. It reestablishes, in the modernist tradition, the connection between the site and the building by utilizing the displaced land to provide a new outdoor space.

Sitting, stair to guest, and living

Master bedroom from study   *Entry from second level*

Benenson Residence

The Benenson residence is on a flat, two-acre site facing Long Island Sound with adjacent structures to the north, east, and west. Like all of the houses since the Cogan residence, this house, though on the mainland, is water related with a primary view to the south; it is object-frame generated and realized; and it has the same orientation and frontality. The site conditions and the split-level parti were similar to the Haupt residence in that the first living level was required to be four feet above grade due to the floodplain. The two-part massing is similar to the Weitz residence; however, in this case the two masses are integrated vertically and horizontally though the entry and the stair.

The entrance, two-car garage, pool terrace, and changing room are located at grade level. Entry is through the porch and hall, up the stairs a half level to the double-height living space and screened porch, dining room, and kitchen. The two children's bedrooms and guest bedroom are located above the garage at the second half-level landing. All of the bedrooms face the view over the pool terrace. Where the guest house in the Weitz residence was connected to the main house through the outdoor stair and interconnecting deck system, the two masses here—the main house and the children's wing—overlap. The interconnection is internal, vertical, and volumetric and reads in section as well as in plan. At the third half landing, a sitting balcony overviews the main living space and is connected to the master bedroom, which overviews the screened porch. The chimney mass, which contains four fireplaces—one each in the main living space, screened porch, sitting balcony, and master bedroom—was the second vertical interlocking element and pivotal reference. The sitting balcony and the chimney mass contribute to the volumetric complexity and elaboration of the primary living space. At the fourth half landing, the last extension of the stair, which, like the chimney mass, extends beyond the frame, accesses a study and roof terrace above the children's wing. The stair is the vertical and horizontal lock between the two wings, acting as a "knuckle" and providing site transitions and different levels of privacy.

The only figural extensions on the exterior are the outdoor deck, the stair and study element, and the circular skylight above the screened porch, which emerges vertically. The main living space is visually and physically extended by both the skylit screened porch and the outside terrace. This was the first time that we used the screened porch as a major indoor/outdoor space. The screened porch was a new volumetric articulation that clearly elaborated and layered the building from the facade as well as extended the interior volume into a defined outdoor room, while simultaneously completing the frame. This strategy was a new elaboration in the house investigation.

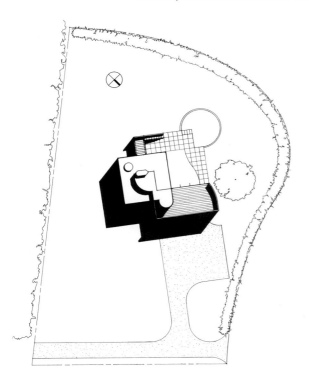

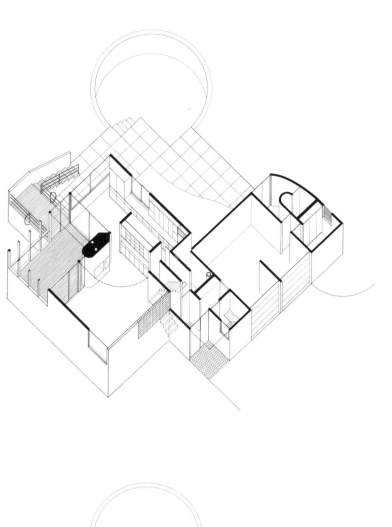
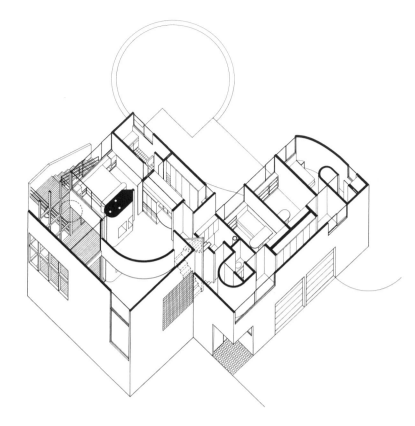
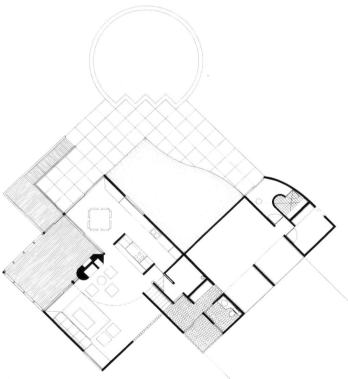
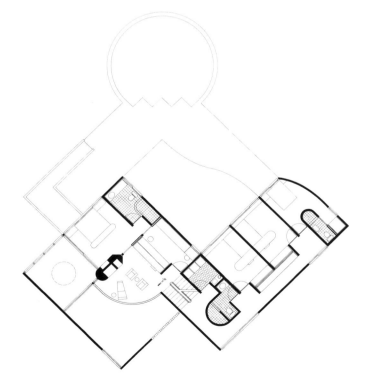

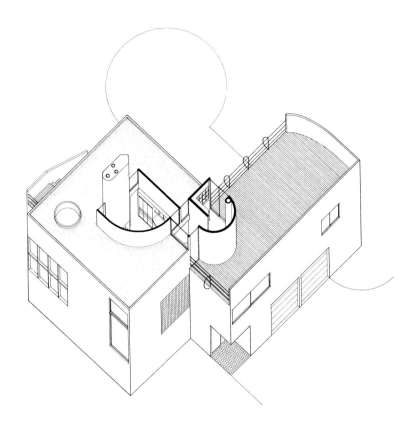

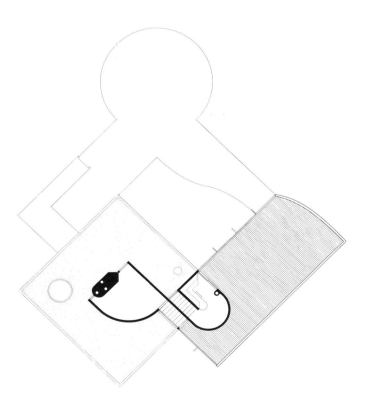

Sitting balcony

Study from stair landing

Bedroom   *Roof deck*

Taft Residence

The Taft residence, on a six-and-a-half-acre site overlooking the Ohio River, consolidated all of the previously discovered strategies. Instead of creating a composite building, here the program is fragmented in response to the client's desire to not have, despite extensive requirements, a "big house." Each of the programmatic elements is distinctly articulated as part of a larger interconnected building/site plan that extends the house and defines a series of outdoor spaces while engaging the landscape.

On approach one reads the frontality of the entry facade as a single element, presenting a frame. The resulting plan configuration is an assemblage of elements, creating a series of volumes and courtyard spaces. This is a three-dimensional object/frame on the landscape. It is the first time that the plan/frame and the volumetric frame are simultaneous. The building and site overlay sequence begins with the entry/auto court, which is defined by a retaining wall and integral greenhouse structure on the north, an arbor on the east, and the entry facade on the south. An opening in the planar entry facade functions as a gateway through which one reads the volume of the building and the depth of the front element as a thick wall. The adjacent courtyard engages the pool house/guest house as a separate element, and is extended by a covered arcade, which connects to the main entrance.

The pool house/guest house, or "children's house," is a two-story element that accommodates living, dining, and kitchen on the ground level and two bedrooms on the second level. The garage element, with two guest rooms on the second level, is located opposite, forming the gateway from the entry court to the main house. The pool terrace, with views south, is located in front of the "children's house," and a grass sculpture garden is located between the garage and the main house.

South facade

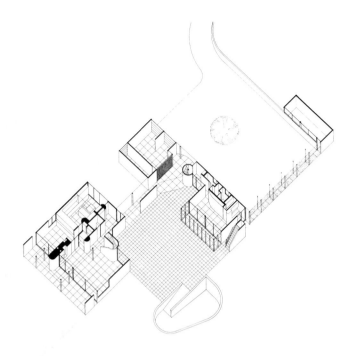

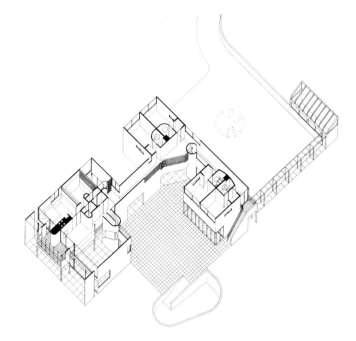

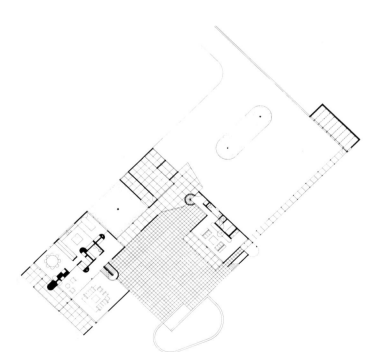

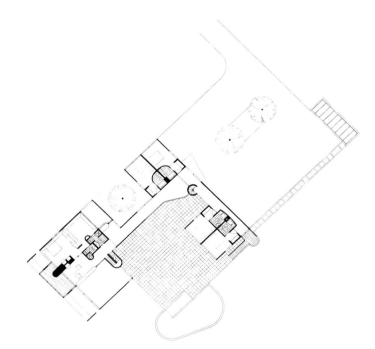

The sequence of arrival is a series of open and covered exterior spaces that unfolds and ultimately brings you to the main house, a single structure that, on the ground level, contains living, dining, kitchen, and breakfast room, and on the second level a master bedroom, study, and balcony/sitting area that opens to a screened porch, which is also an extension of the master bedroom. On the third level is a roof deck, another major outdoor space that overviews the entire composition. This was the "small house" the Taft's had requested.

On the second level, over the outdoor entry arcade , a linear gallery connects the main house to the two guest bedrooms in the "children's house" and to the two guest rooms above the garage. This sense of separation and connection on the family level allows everyone to feel that they have their own private domain while simultaneously being part of a whole.The one-and-a-half-story gallery features a curved glass block wall and, as a space, is transitional, connective, and primary. Operating as a spine, the gallery becomes the connector through the site, through the building, and reveals the framed views as one moves sequentially through the layered elements.

The culmination of this progression is the south-facing sunscreen, which is an integrated extension of the living/dining space on the ground level and the screen porch on the second level. The sunscreen is articulated as a separate volumetric layer at the edge, presenting both transparency and depth. It is a precursor to the denser and more complex layering of the de Menil residence, and marks the beginning of the next discovery process that involves more complex layering with walls reading as space as opposed to plane.

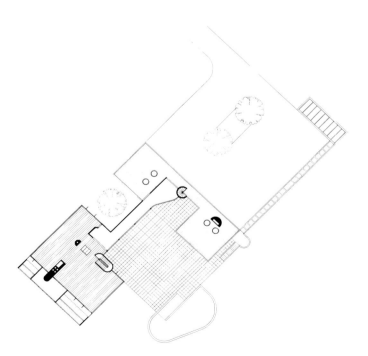

View from terrace   **195**

Living and gallery balcony

Gallery and guest sitting

Study

View from southeast (overleaf) **201**

de Menil Residence

The de Menil residence involved developing seven acres on a private dune site, with access from the north, dense woods on the east and west, and a half-mile-deep dune and ocean to the south. The response represents a reconsolidation of the programmatic elements that were separated in the Taft residence and an extended investigation of buildings as objects that create a dialogue between one another and inform landscape transitions.

The arrival sequence begins with the driveway passing through the woods and a gate. Turning west, a pink stucco wall seemingly floats in a half-acre pond, a landscaped water element in counterpoint to the ocean beyond. Turning south, one passes through the stucco wall. On axis with the cobblestone drive, flanked on the west by a row of linden trees, is a long view to the ocean, a total site reference framed and abstracted by the exterior stair, brise soleil, and pool wall of the main house. Continuing down the drive and passing the colored stucco guest house/garage, an extension of the entry wall fragment, the full facade of the main house is finally revealed from the auto court. These three elements—the gate, the guest house, and the pool wall—comprise the series of outdoor fragments that asymmetrically establish the site architecture framing the main house.

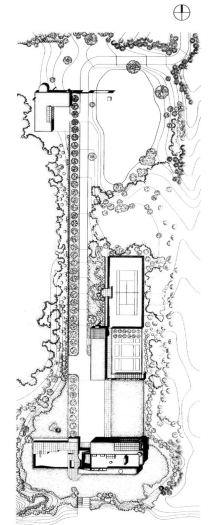

The house crosses the axis of the driveway and is parallel to the ocean, mediating between the land and dune sides of the site. The main facades face north, back to the property, and south, to the dunes and ocean. In plan, the house is layered north to south, in a series of four articulated and modulated zones—entry/ greenhouse, circulation (the east-west organizer of the site), living, and sunscreen/brise soleil. One is constantly aware of these zones, their internal facades as well as their spatial transparency and layering. The sequential transition of spaces establishes the idea of volume as wall rather than plane as wall, a new dimension in our residential work.

Entering the house through a two-story entry erosion, one is aware of the volume and presence of the greenhouse through which other interior spaces are revealed. The greenhouse is the interior garden, the extension and resolution of

View from southeast over dunes

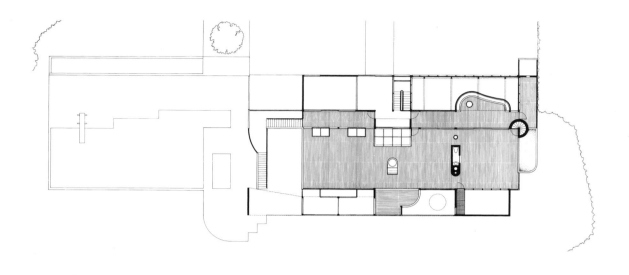

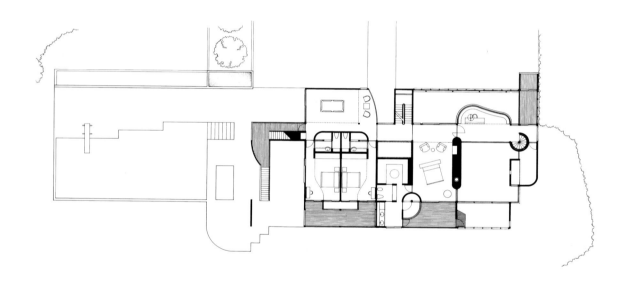

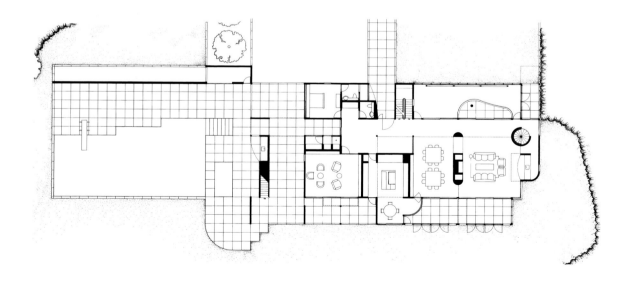

the landscape sequence—tennis court, garden, arbor, lawn—within the volume of the house. The three-and-a-half-story greenhouse is perceived as the major volume from the exterior and interior, a frame modulated by the intervention of a study balcony as an object. The sequence of outdoor spaces, and their extension/ integration into and through the house, unifies the site and the building.

The entry gallery is the three-story-high, skylit, cross-axial space of the circulation zone. To the right is the library, with a terrace opening to the view. Straight ahead is the kitchen/ breakfast room, which is literally and programmatically the center of the house, serving the library, library terrace, screened porch, and dining room. To the left is the dining room, separated from the two-story living room by the green stucco fireplace/chimney mass, which anchors the house to the site and recalls the site walls. Both spaces are contained within and simultaneously defined and extended by the facades and volumes of the greenhouse and screened porch.

The second-floor gallery is a balcony overviewing the entry hall. To the right is the guest suite, which contains two guest rooms and decks, with views to the ocean, and a game room with its own exterior stair down to the pool terrace. To the left is the master bedroom suite including sitting, dressing, and sleeping areas as well as a master bath with a deck that is integrated into the brise soleil. Past the master bedroom, the gallery overviews the living room and expands into the study, the object in the frame of the greenhouse.

On the third level, the study loft overviews the game room, which opens to the upper level of the greenhouse. Both spaces open directly to the roof, a major outdoor space that resolves the building vertically. The chimney, skylights, and greenhouse are articulated forms that recall the spaces below, while the views of the dunes and ocean, framed by the brise soleil, recall the bridge of an ocean liner.

The brise soleil, the south facade layer, has been incorporated into the organization of the house instead of being a separate element. It is a frame that accommodates a series of objects—the screened porch, the breakfast room, the master bathroom, and a series of terraces and decks. It reads as a cornice to the site, a major scale device that establishes its presence as a piece of architecture. Like the earlier dune houses of the Hamptons, it is large enough to anchor the site and coexist with the scale of the dunes and the ocean.

The de Menil residence marks the beginning of the second phase of my career. It is both a summary and the initiation of a new level of complexity and integration. It extends the object/frame investigation initiated in the Cogan house as well as the volumetric and layering investigation initiated in the Taft house. In de Menil, multiple frames are interlocked and engaged by the extension of spaces from one into the other, reinforcing the volumetric content. This is further reinforced as one moves vertically through the house and experiences the sectional manipulation. Though simple in plan, the section is dense and varied. The design intuitions are referential to my parents' house in that they were implanted and manifested without excessive intellectual refinements or manipulations. They have a freshness and a primary essence that is unadulterated, making this building pertinent to the ongoing creative process.

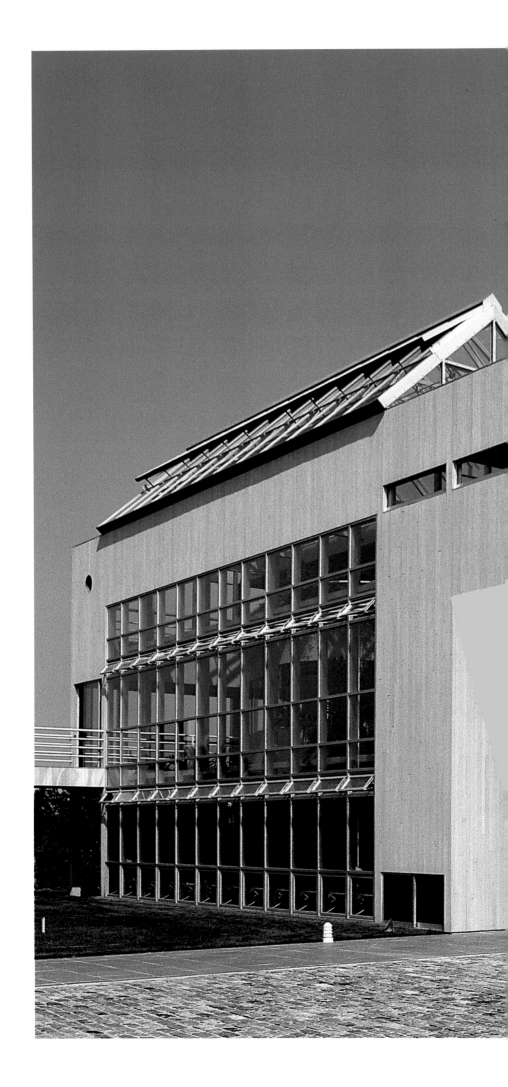

Entry gate   Guest house from drive

View from northwest

Pool from roof deck   *West facade*

Brise soleil and porch toward auto court and guest house

View from roof deck

Detail of east facade

Entry

Detail of south facade

Kitchen and breakfast room

226   *Detail of stair*

Second-level gallery

Game room

228   *Master bedroom sitting area*

Second-level gallery from balcony study

Balcony study from greenhouse　　　　　　　　*North facade (overleaf)*　　**233**

Viereck Residence

The Viereck residence came into the office while the de Menil residence was under construction and was an anomaly in terms of scale. It was the size of the earlier, pre-Taft houses. The clients were a French photographer and his German wife, a graphic designer who had incredible visual sensibilities and precision. They had a European point of view about space and privacy—or lack of it—which was very different from the typical American sensibility. There was no question about the viability of modernism and the idea of abstraction and reductiveness.

The parti, organizationally, is very similar to my parents' house. The ground floor accomodates a three-story entry and stair space, two guest rooms, a garage, and a studio with views to the east. The second level accomodates a two-story living/dining space, a kitchen, and a master bedroom—all opening to a deck extension overviewing the wooded, six-acre site and a panoramic view of Gardner's Bay. The third level accomodates a balcony/sitting room, overviewing the living/dining space, with an adjacent roof deck.

The spaces in the house are a collection of loft environments of varying sizes where each element becomes an object integrated into a frame. The revelation of this house is that one is constantly aware of the two-story living space as the primary volume anchoring the vertical volumetric consolidation, with the section determining the privacy zones.

In the previous houses, the exterior and interior had always been simultaneous. Even when the two were of different materials, they were treated consistently with regard to color—white. At the insistence of the client, this was the first time that the exterior cedar siding was natural and the interior was white. It was as if the cedar had been carved into, exposing a different veining. The transformation of the previous aesthetic and the re-evaluation of the preconception—that the outside and the inside were the same or simultaneous—was an exploratory revelation for me.

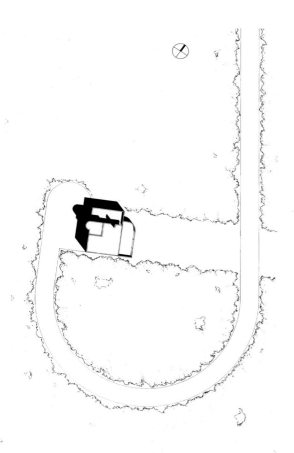

View from northwest

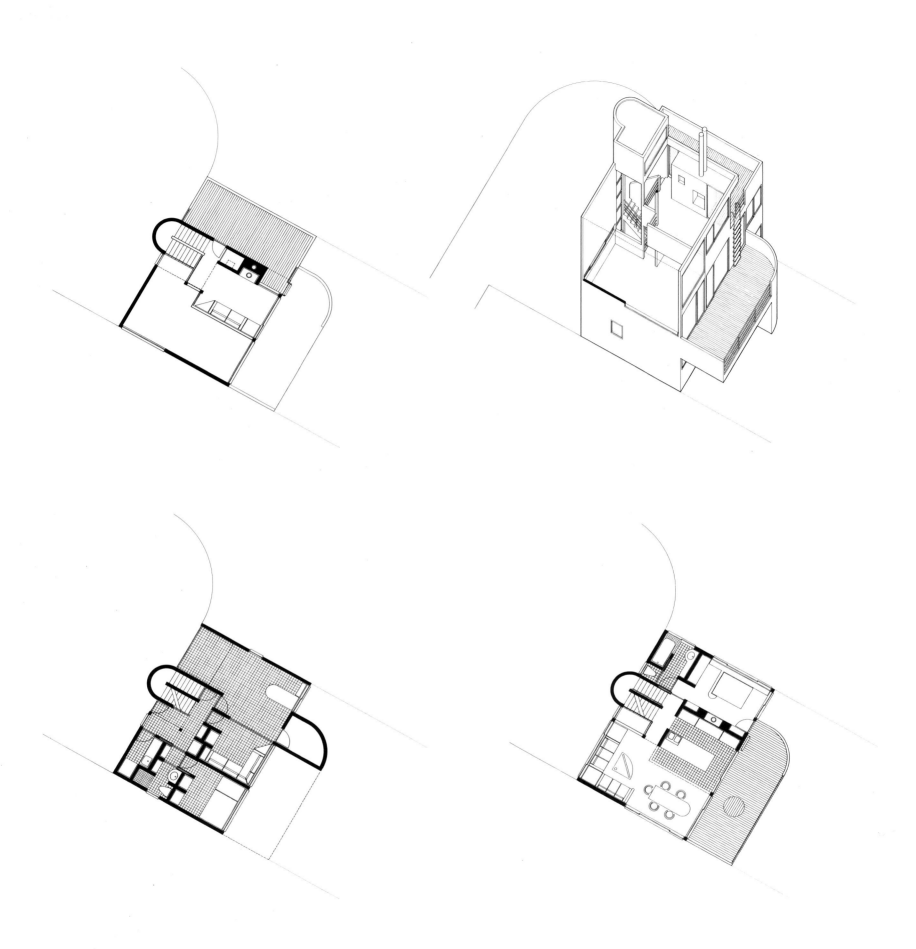

Ground, second, and third level plans and axonometric

Southeast facade

View from south

Stair from living

Living and dining to stair

Garey Residence

Designed as an object in the woods, the Garey residence is sequentially revealed by a site and building circulation system that culminates in the glass-enclosed, cylindrical living space. The route leads through the sloping twenty-seven-acre site, into the house, and eventually back out to the landscape, with views of a mountain stream and forest. The house becomes a site mediator, with the massing changing from solid (public) to void (private), and the split-level plan responding to the topographic shifts in the landscape, reinforcing the dialogue between architecture and nature.

The parti is formally related to the Benenson residence in that there is a main house element with a perpendicular children's house/garage wing, and a "knuckle" connection—the entry and stair—between the two masses. Of all the split-level houses with similar organizations, this is the most consistent and interlocked. Every space, transition, and intersection is literally engaged and reinforced by the stair and the stair landings. The stair becomes the vertical spatial integrator and the plan organizer of the parti.

The lower ground floor accommodates the entry and garage. The upper ground floor, a half level above, contains the kitchen/dining area, the sitting room, and the two-and-a-half-story main living space. Over the garage, a half level above the living area, is the two-bedroom children's wing. Another half level above, overviewing the main living space, is the master bedroom suite. The stair terminates another half level above in an ascendant interior space, which is the private study at the top of the building, with an adjacent major roof terrace over the children's wing which overlooks both the stream and a pool.

The pool is a plan extension of the children's wing, located a level below the entry, adjacent to the stream. The man-made body of water is in counterpoint to the natural water, but is not visible in the primary views from any of the living spaces—so as not to compromise or contaminate the views of the stream and the woods.

The primary living space, a glass rotunda, is the iconic form of the building. This is the first time that a cylindrical volume is introduced as an intervention into the orthogonal organization. The form of the rotunda extends from the outside into the house and becomes the wall and the ceiling figure of the master bedroom and the study below. It is superimposed on the orthogonal grid, forming a bay window at a non-traditional scale. The gridded fenestration continues from the exterior through the interior, rendering the master bedroom acoustically private but visually integrated into the living room and the site. The transparency of the volume, rather than simply the skin, extends the ideas initially investigated in the de Menil residence, where wall as space, rather than plane, reinforced both spatial layering and density.

The materiality of the house becomes an extended and integrated palette of natural materials: cedar siding, inside and out; mahogany windows, doors, and cabinets; and slate floors. Rather than relying on a palette of abstract materials, the selection of these natural materials, with their inherent textures and color, enriches and reinforces the hierarchical strategies integral to the architecture.

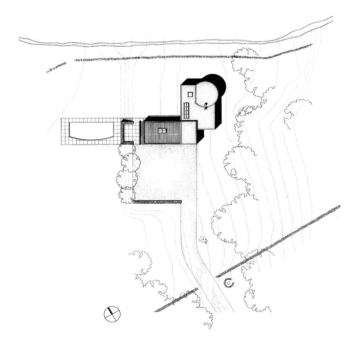

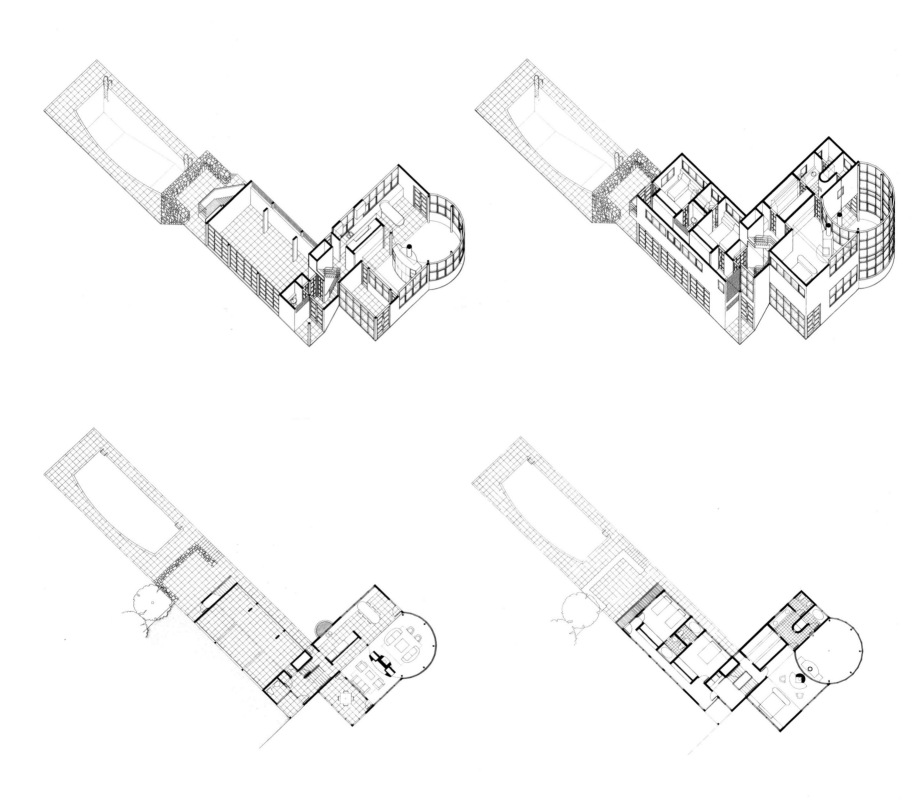

Ground/first, second/third, and roof level plans and axonometrics

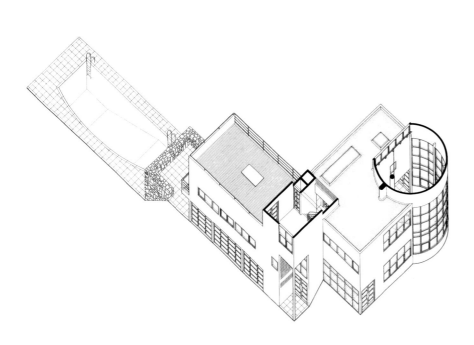

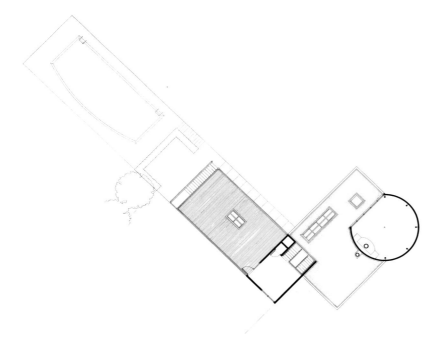

Detail of southwest facade

Detail of southeast facade   *View from east*

Study/library

Living and dining   *Detail of stair*   *Kitchen and dining* **257**

Guest bedroom

Master bedroom sitting area   Master bedroom   Master bath

Spielberg Residence

We were working with Steven on an apartment in New York City when he purchased this piece of land in East Hampton. He already had a house designed for the site by a California architect, but was unsure, and asked me if I would design a house for him on this site. His one stipulation was that it had to be "traditional." I told him we don't do traditional houses. I tried to think of how we could get together aesthetically and philosophically. The site was spectacular—a beautiful field on the edge of Georgica Pond, a major water intervention into the East Hampton landscape, with a view to the ocean.

I proposed the idea of finding an old barn and using the frame as a generator and a precedent in establishing the figure and the volume as well as the organizing device for planning the house. This idea was intriguing to Steven because it allowed him to get over the "traditional/modern" problem, and was intriguing to me because of the possibility of transformation. We found a Dutch barn, which had a perfect configuration—a center volume and side aisles, the latter being the stalls, and the former being the storage and work space. We built a foundation and erected the 52-foot-square-by-31-foot-high frame on the site.

The strategy of the transformation was to maintain the structural and volumetric integrity of the frame on the interior. The frame is revealed to be the memory and the graphic trace of the "historic" barn. The exposed frame and infilled stucco walls create a half-timbered "exterior" reading. The exterior was sheathed in a thick shingle wall, retaining the barn's iconic volume while transforming its scale and image to a more abstract vernacular. The windows, instead of being surface-mounted, which is typical of traditional shingle architecture, are deeply recessed, articulating the tension between the idea of skin versus wall. A front porch and cylinder were added to the original frame, simultaneously layering and extending the space.

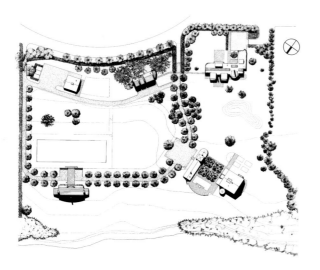

The barn, as the initial structure, became the generator for the extended site plan, which, over time, incorporated six structures on eleven acres. The first building one encounters upon entering the site is the gatehouse, which becomes the mediator between the public side of the site and the private side. One drives into the site and approaches the gatehouse diagonally. It is a long, low building separating the auto court from the courtyard, which is defined by sixteen pear trees and is frontal to the barn and cross-axial to the site and pond. Both the auto court and the courtyard reflect the plan dimension of the barn and create a spatial sequence that culminates in the main volume.

The completed six buildings—two guest houses, a stable, and the caretaker's house in addition to the original barn and gatehouse—all interact across a landscape that has been designed as an integral part of the architectural experience. There is a multiplicity of scales—structures, the riding ring, lawns facing the pond, the defined lawns between the building. The buildings are familial but not imitative of each other. This has been an exploration of how objects can be sited so that they participate yet maintain their singularity and privacy, all of which takes cues from the original parti, but extends it. If, in the beginning, we had known there would be six buildings on this site, the result would have been very different. The fact that this process was sequential and unexpected, and that the addition of each site and each building caused us to reconsider and reintegrate the whole, forced us to discover strategies that I don't think we would have come to so clearly. Each new program, each new idea, enriched, elaborated, and informed the whole.

The proof, for me, of the strength of the barn as architecture and as a generator for all of the subsequent work was seeing it just completed, with no furniture. It was a powerful graphic element overlaid on a clear spatial organization. The inherent quality of the frame, its order and its hierarchical structure, was irrefutable. There was an umcontaminated strength about its singularity, both formally and literally. As a modern architect, dealing with the "constraint" of this rigorous subtext was a unique, though tangential, investigation. I have been asked if it is contradictory to our ideology. I don't think it is because it was not conceived as a stylistic problem, but as a formal investigation of how to exploit an "existing condition," one which we introduced and then transformed. It was, as at Whig Hall in Princeton, a matter of accepting the "found object" and using it as the generator for the investigation and the solution—as opposed to "making it." Since the "found object" had a rigorous organization and a volumetric clarity, it was already a part of our ethic and was, from that point of view, not contradictory.

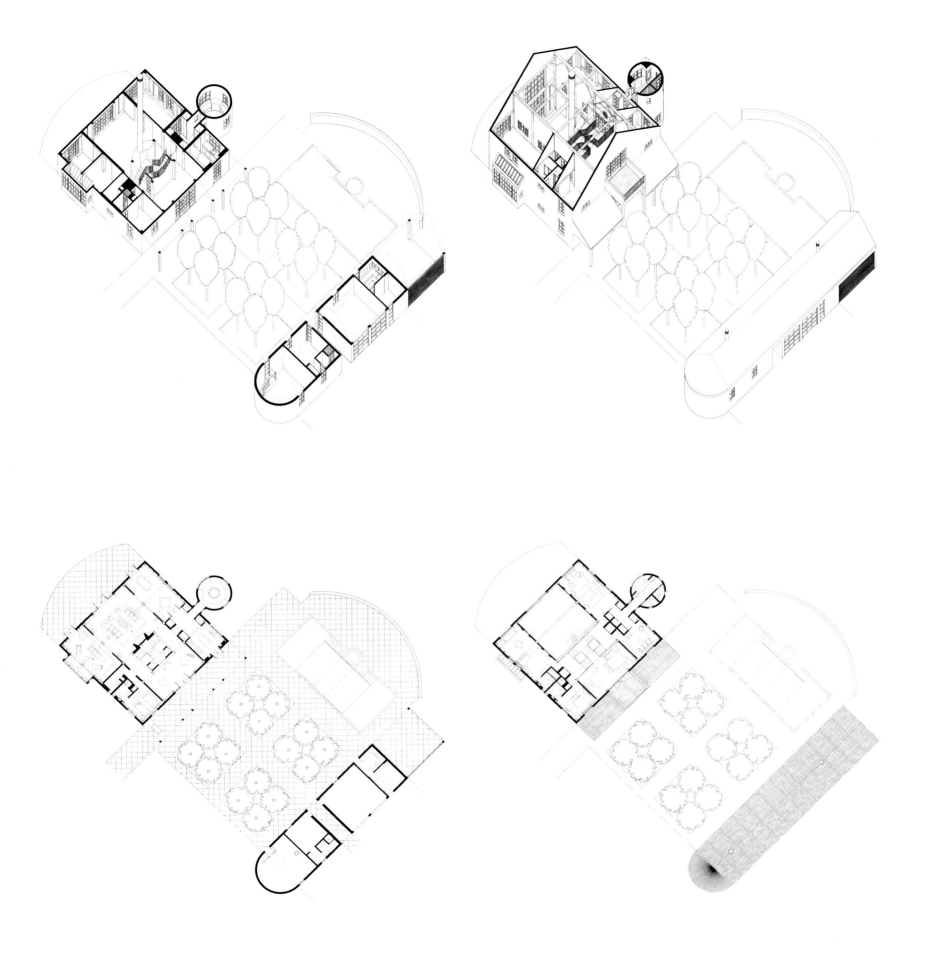

Ground and second level plans and axonometrics of barn and gate house

Gate house and barn from pond (overleaf)

View of gate house and barn from northeast

Courtyard to east facade of barn

Detail of master bath   *Detail from northwest*   *Master bath*   *Breakfast room from kitchen*

Opel Residence

The Opel residence is sited on a twelve-acre, wooded peninsula—part of the old Vanderbilt estate on Lake Champlain—with panoramic views north and west across and down the lake to the Adirondack Mountains. The clients, a retired couple who had children and grandchildren, wanted to be able to accommodate all three generations in the building. Instead of designing a single house that consolidated these different programmatic requirements, we designed a series of interconnected pavilions that allowed privacy and multiple uses.

The parti, an elaboration of the "gallery/spine" concept incubated in the Taft residence, is both program- and site-specific—it separates the guest and children's areas from the main house and affords varying lake views from all living spaces. These elements are organized along an arcade and are visually interconnected through a series of courtyard spaces. In section, the arcade is carved or eroded, rather than additive. It is cut under the second level and is terminated by the entry to the main house. It engages the different elements of the house and the exterior spaces, intensifying the overall experience of the architecture.

The linear spatial sequence is initiated at the auto court with the entry at the south end of the spine. To access the arcade one passes between the garage and the stair to the children's "bunk house"—a large, linear, open space over the garage that the children could, over time, adjust and remake as their own environment. Walking down the arcade, one passes, sequentially, a lakeside opening that accesses the pool terrace, the caretaker's apartment, and a garden/landside opening, with the two "guest house" entrances opposite, before arriving at the entry to the main house.

The "guest houses," modeled on a European studio prototype, each contain an entry stair/hall off the arcade, a kitchen, and a two-and-a-half-story living/dining space with a vaulted roof and glazed facade that faces the lake and accommodates a fireplace/chimney object. Adjacent to each of these spaces is a private courtyard also facing the lake. The sleeping balcony overviews the living space and the lake.

The main house, on the ground level, contains a double-height entry hall, a kitchen/breakfast space, dining and a two-and-a-half-story living space, similar to, though larger than, the guest houses. One half level above is a studio, and on the second level is the master bedroom suite, both overviewing the living room and the lake.

The section of the main house is a more complex and elaborated version of the "guest houses." All read as pavilions, with the underside of the vaulted roof being the space definer. The parabolic curve of the standing-seam metal roof creates the universal silhouette of the house. This curve is extended the length of the building and then cut into segments, leaving discrete elements that are visually connected by a continuous gutter element that establishes a frame for the lakeside facade.

Simultaneously, the rhythm of the three fireplaces and chimneys acts as a vertical counterpoint to the curved roof and gutter forms. They are the stabilizing elements in the glass facades and allow the furniture to be oriented toward both the view and the fireplace. By placing the fireplaces within the glass facade, they become animated elements in a richer and larger composition that engages the landscape, lake, and mountains instead of being isolated foci and anachronistic elements in the space. From a formal and architectural point of view, their placement anchors both the space and the building.

The silhouette of the building is read on approach and is a contextual reinterpretation of the barns on the property and their animated roof silhouettes. The idea of silhouette, rather than the specific silhouette, became the generator. The variation and the dynamic that results from the sequence of solid and void confirm the sense of expectation and reinforces a reading of the house as a village, establishing itself on the end of the point and simultaneously engaging the lakefront and the memory of the farm.

This is a cedar house using natural stone site walls and a zinc roof as counterpoints. It extends the natural palette initiated in the Garey residence—mahogany windows and doors, cedar siding, slate floors, stone, and zinc. Each material has its own texture, scale, and color. Individually and together, the materials substantiate the architecture.

View from drive to northeast

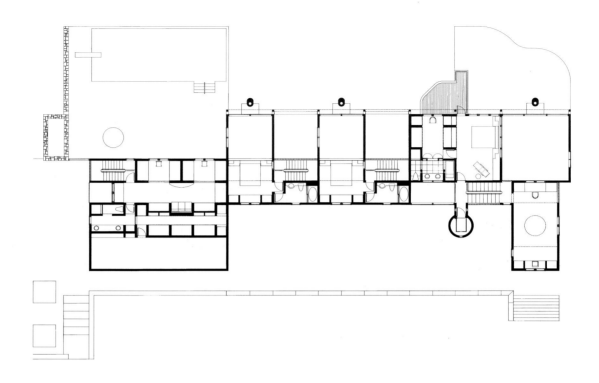

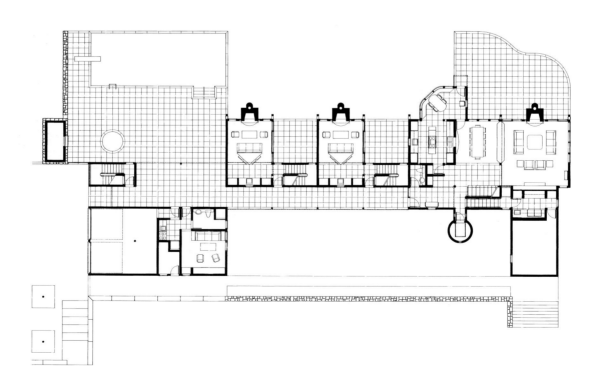

282   Ground and second level plans

Detail of south facade from auto court   *Entry arcade*

Detail of guest pavilion, west facade

Guest pavilion dining and living

Dining, living, and stair from entry

Detail of studio

Master bedroom   Dressing   Master bath

Detail of west facade and courtyard

West facade (overleaf)

Gimelstob Residence

The Gimelstob residence sits on a seventeen-acre meadow modulated by a longitudinal ridge with a ten-foot grade change running east to west at the rear of the site. Instead of "centering" the house in the meadow and approaching it frontally, which would be the traditional strategy, the house is located on the ridge, anchoring it to the land. Because of the grade change, the building is both on as well as in the land—sited on the meadow and across the slope. The topographic change was a found condition and became the primary generator for the parti.

Like the Taft residence, this is a large house that is articulated as a series of separate volumes that engage the land and establish a sense of place by defining a series of outdoor spaces. The formal investigation focused on how a program can be articulated through a separation and reconsolidation of the parts through an interlocked and composite manipulation of both plan and section. Instead of pulling the program apart, as in the Taft residence, the section, not the plan, is used to create the site integration.

The drive comes around the house and slopes down a full level to the autocourt and garage—what had initially been perceived as a two-story house is now revealed as three stories. One enters at the lower ground level or ascends a major exterior stair that returns to the meadow level of the main house. The living space is a double-height rotunda first realized in the Garey residence. In this case, the rotunda is encapsulated, becoming the central and centroidal organizing space. It is geometric, iconic, and skylit, establishing the presence of the building on the site. It is an exploration of geometric erosion that results in the figural and articulated solid/void manipulation of the space itself.

On the ground level of the rotunda is the living room, flanked by a sitting area and a dining space, as well as the kitchen/breakfast room, which opens to the pool terrace. On the upper level, the rotunda is articulated by a circulation balcony that overviews the living room and looks through the space. On either side of the balcony, above the sitting area and above the dining room, is the library and the master bedroom suite, both overviewing the main living space.

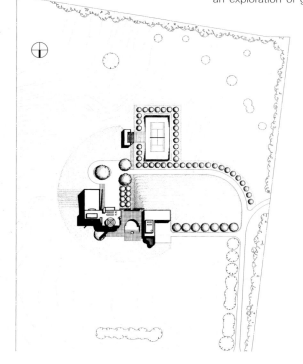

North facade

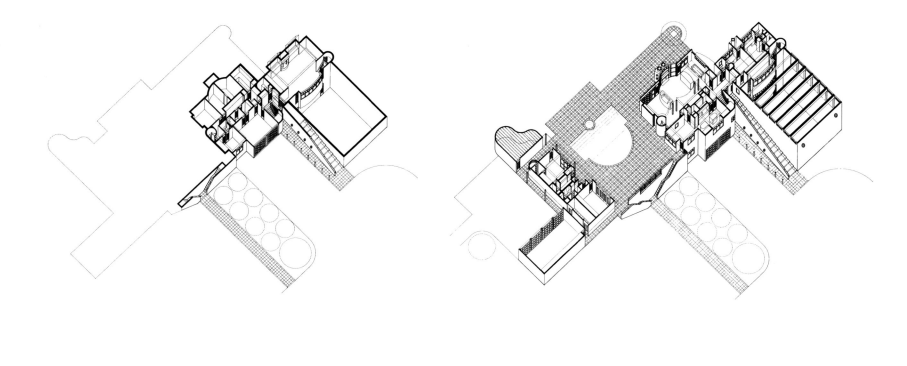

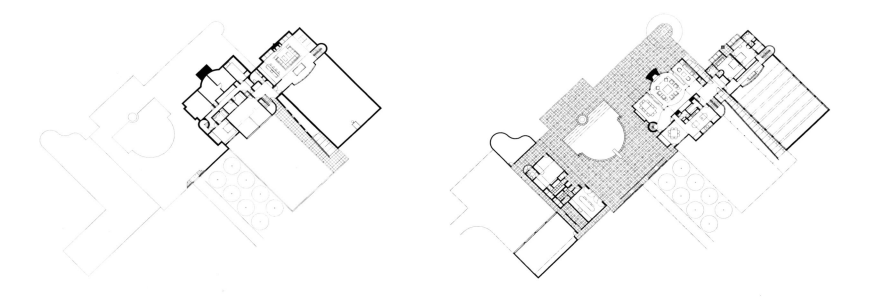

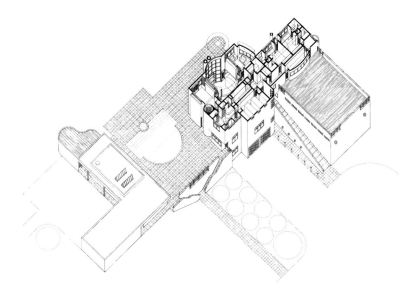

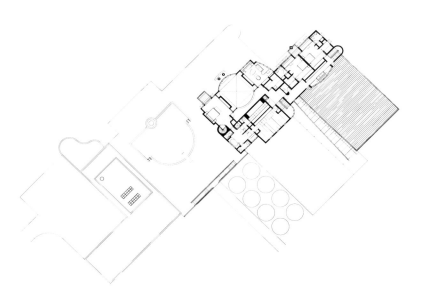

The far side of the pool terrace is defined by a single-story pool house, garage, and guest suite. On the south, the courtyard is defined by a site retaining wall, which overviews the lower ground level and is connected to the tennis court by a site stair and path that extends through the pear tree courtyard.

The "children's house" is articulated as its own wing. It is a four-story building set into the ground, reducing its perceived volume and anchoring the entire composition. It has its own organization as well as its own internal circulation system. There are two levels of children's bedrooms accessed by circulation galleries: the upper-level gallery opens to a major roof deck, facing south, the lower-level gallery overviews the gymnasium space. Underneath the lower-level gallery and bedrooms, also overviewing the gymnasium, is the gameroom. There is a dense vertical stacking and sectional complexity that is not revealed from either side of the site. As one descends, the spaces become larger, wider, and unexpected—a reverse sequence to the main house.

The parti of using the house as a site wall that acts as a filter was first explored in a number of our earlier dune houses—the Cohn, Haupt, and Weitz residences—but this is the first time that the section of the site became the organizing section of the building. Seeing the house across the meadow and then arriving one level lower and returning to the meadow level via the main house reengages the site and establishes a dynamic memory sequence—the house is not just an object but a sequential, mediating, vertical/horizontal bridge on the landscape.

View from northwest

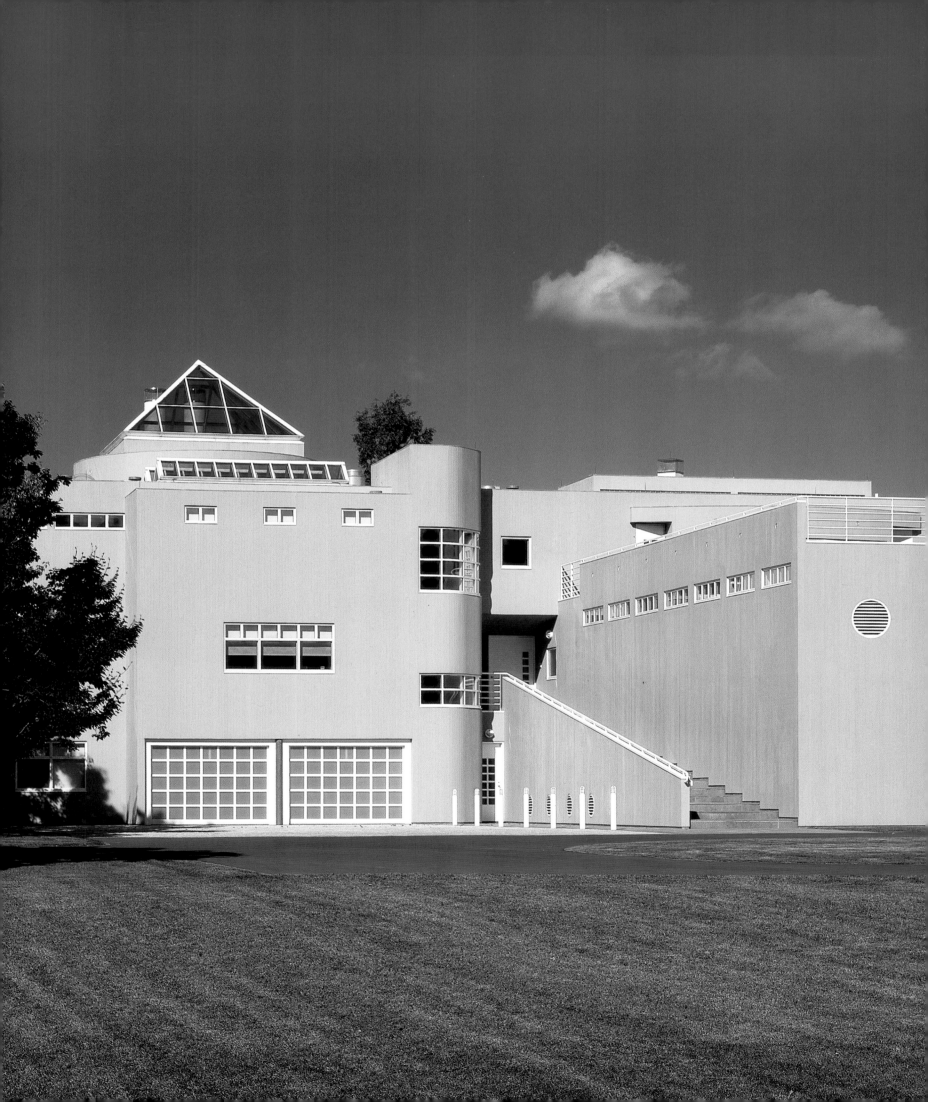

Dining, living, and sitting from gallery

Kitchen Breakfast room

Living

Master bedroom

Master bedroom

Game room   *Gymnasium*

Oceanfront Residence

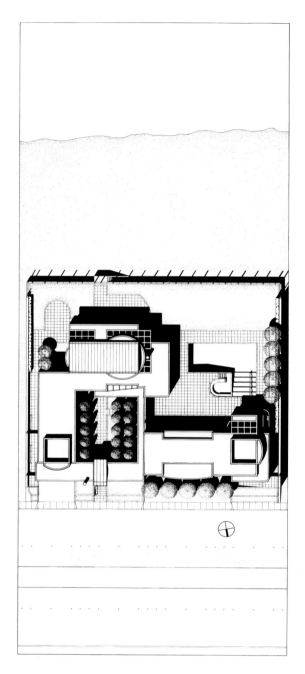

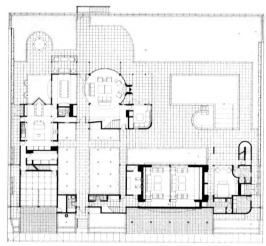

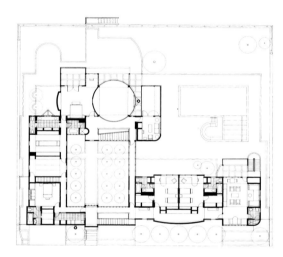

The Oceanfront residence was the first of our California houses to be realized. The 150-foot-wide-by-100-foot-deep site is defined by the Pacific Coast Highway on the north and the Pacific Ocean on the south. The house is adjacent to a six-lane highway and only 100 feet from the Pacific Ocean. The parti combines the row house and the courtyard house typologies, creating a hierarchy of building volumes and outdoor spaces that layer the site from north to south, resulting in a literal and psychological transformation from highway to beach.

The highway facade of the entry building is the first layer on the site. It is primarily solid, rendered as a carved, abstract horizontal wall punctured by an entry gate. It is an acoustical barrier, separating the rest of the site from the road. Its depth and its density, as well as its program, shield the site from the acoustic intrusion. On the ground level, the entry building houses a screening room, guest house, garage, and pool support space. On the second level are two children's bedrooms, a playroom, and a caretaker's apartment over the garage.

As a linear, horizontal figure, the facade of the entry building, with its three-dimensional modulations and articulations, suggests the presence of the different programmatic elements housed within, while simultaneously presenting a large-scale, abstract "road graphic." It is specific without being revealing; it is designed as a response to both the highway and to itself. The facade is not about singular frontality, but rather linear, sixty-mile-per-hour frontality where the articulated incidents that occur along it are intended to be perceived as a progression. It is only when you park that there is the opportunity to visually and literally penetrate the wall frontally.

One passes through the entry building from the gate to a courtyard conceived as a vestibule to the main house. The courtyard is planted with three rows of five pear trees that flank the path from the gate to the front door of the main house. The courtyard is defined on the east by the second site layer, a building that contains the kitchen, pantry, and breakfast room on the ground level and a master bathroom, dressing room, and exercise space on the second level. A bridge that connects the children's wing to the main house on the second level defines the courtyard on the west.

The main house, the third site layer, contains living, dining, library, and porch on the ground level. On the second level a master bedroom, study and decks face the ocean and overview the cylindrical double-height living space—the primary interior volume and the primary referential space of the composition. It engages all of the outdoor spaces as well as the ocean, and becomes the mediator between the private domain and the public domains of the site. The space establishes the cross axis of the site.

From the courtyard one enters the main house as well as the pool terrace, under a bridge, establishing a diagonal sequence of exterior spaces that are separate but interconnected. The entry court is defined on three sides, the pool terrace is defined on two sides by the entry building and the main house, as well as the front lawn, an extended horizontal plane that runs the full 150-foot width of the site.

Passing through this series of sequential indoor/outdoor spaces, the facades on the ocean side open up to the view and become more transparent, as opposed to solid. There is a transformation of facades—the north/road facade is closed and articulated as solid, the south/ocean facade is open and articulated as void. The idea was to establish separate elements that are programmatically articulate and engage the entire site. The site plan and the building plan are simultaneous and result in a composition that is composite, where the inside and outside spaces are integrated.

The rotunda space is the primary figural public room, yet it is different from similar spaces in the Garey and Gimelstob residences in that it is totally encapsulated in and revealed as an object that has been carved from the overall frame. The space is experienced as having been found within the frame of the overall site rather than as a singular, articulate volume.

This house is similar to the Taft parti in that the program has been pulled apart and reassembled. But, unlike Taft, it was less an assemblage and more a whole that was then carved away, leaving exterior spaces—the "found" spaces, the spaces between the architectural figures that are as elemental and primary as the forms that define them. It is as if we took this entire site and covered it with a two-story block and started carving away. The process . is subtractive, not additive. What is left of the "excavation" are the essential elements that were formed by the exploration of subtraction. The result is one of revealing essence and an enriched integration of parts that form a composite whole.

Living, stair, and balcony   **331**

Gallery balcony and stair

Bridge

Children's gallery from north stair landing

Detail of screening room

Detail of south facade

Detail of east facade

Zumikon Residence

The Zumikon residence is, to date, our only house in Europe. The clients, major art collectors, were incredibly acute and regarded modernism as a critical period in the history of architecture. There was never a debate about the aesthetic. The section and the organization of the house were informed by a stringent building code: the square footage of the house (excluding underground areas) was limited to a proportional relationship to the area of the site, the existing topography had to be retained, and the roofline could not exceed four and a half meters above the corresponding point in the land. Given the sloping site, the house became a truly site-integrated building.

The house engages the land and steps up the hill, evolving into a series of interconnected pavilions. This assemblage forms a "village" that anchors and establishes an overall site/building context. There is, simultaneously, a deconsolidation, where each element is distinctly articulated, and a reconsolidation, where the building, anchored by two vertical circulation elements and a horizontal connecting gallery, becomes denser and more composite as the sequence is revealed.

The front element engages the lower ground with a garage and entry. The second level, accessed by an outdoor stair from the entry court as well as by a service drive and court, contains the breakfast room and kitchen and is connected to a perpendicular horizontal pavilion. On the ground level, below grade, is an art gallery, integrated into the entry/circulation sequence of the house. The gallery, a linear columned space, connects the two-and-a-half-story front entry hall to the rear stair. The front stair connects the lower entry level to the main living level, one story above. The entry space establishes, under the curved, segmented roof form, the volumetric ethic of the house and engages one vertically and horizontally, revealing the diagram of the house.

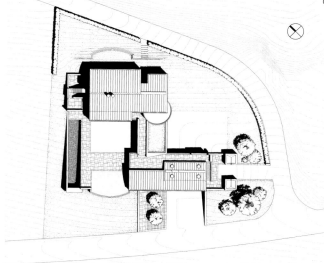

View from southwest

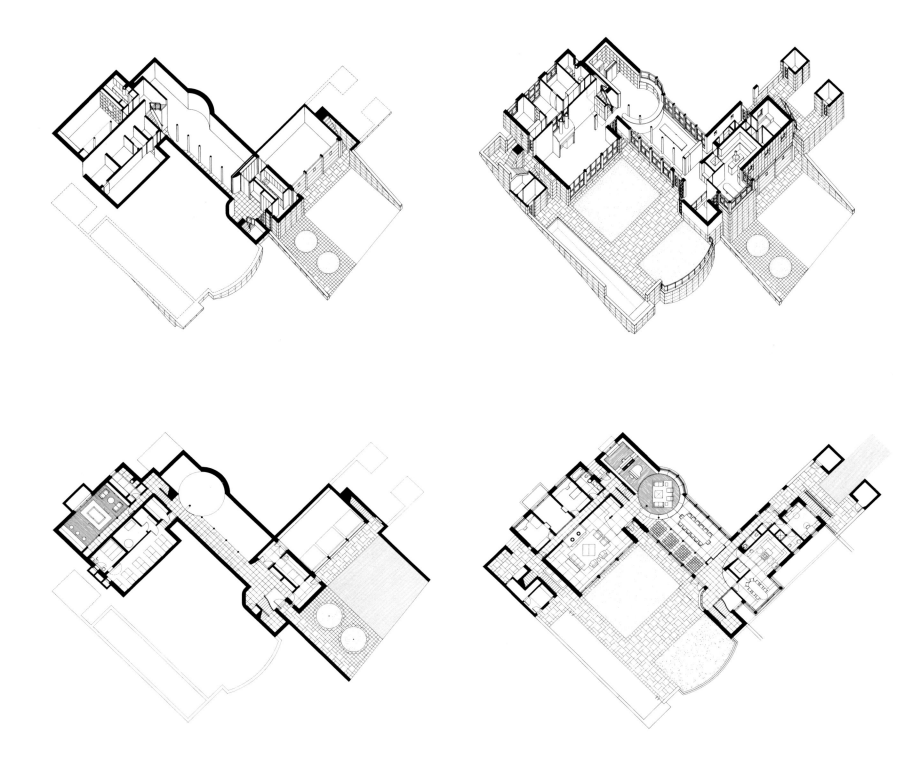

Lower, second, third, and roof level plans and axonometrics

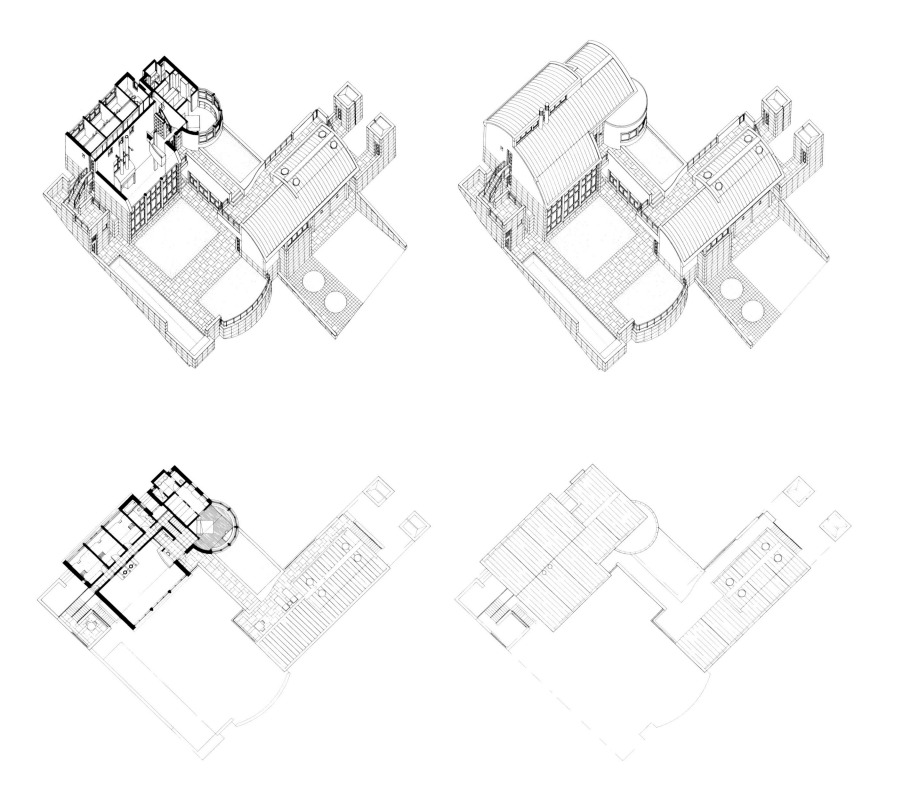

On the second level of the pavilion is the dining room, which serves as a transparent mediator between the natural topography of the sloped site on the east and the integrated courtyard on the west. The glass-block floor brings natural light into the gallery below and, with the concrete columns, articulates the circulation zone. The roof of the dining room becomes a garden terrace off the master bedroom above. A three-story cylindrical form marks the intersection of the horizontal pavilion and the main house. The cylinder contains the terminal space of the gallery on the ground floor, the music room/library on the second floor, and the master bedroom on the third floor. It is the formal device that allows the main house to rotate 90 degrees and is a critical spatial recognition of the intersection.

The double-height living space opens toward the main terrace and the view of Lake Zurich and the Alps beyond. It is the terminal space in a circulation sequence that is hierarchical, volumetrically complex, and site revealing. When one finally arrives at the main living space, the entire site/house relationship is comprehended. It is the interior space that is in scale with both the terrace and the view. The fireplace wall of the living room is the front wall to the three-story children's house, which is accessed as a separate vertical building at the half-landings of the rear stair, separating it from the main public and adult levels. At the lowest half level, off the art gallery, is a double-height playroom. Two bedrooms flank this space on the second level, and an additional three bedrooms are located on the third level. Each of these levels is connected by a gallery that overlooks the living room through punched windows, allowing the children to see through the living room to the view beyond. The children have their own entrance as well as their own interconnection to the main terrace through the two galleries, which also access the roof terrace of the pool pavillion.

The opportunity to build this house of reinforced concrete with the level of craft that exists in Switzerland was compelling and influenced the form. This is literally a building of the ground, with a density and sense of permanence that is entirely different from that of our wood-frame houses. The materials used in this house—stucco on terra cotta walls; lead-coated stainless steel roofs; wood windows and cabinetry; limestone, sandstone and wood floors—produced a selective aesthetic that is precise, hierarchical, and self-decorative.

There is nothing automatic about the vocabulary, either materially or formally. The curved, segmented roofs of the Opel residence provide a sectional reference. Though articulated as separate volumes, they are read as one form. In this house, however, the roofs vary and are more dynamic due to the elements that intersect them, causing variations and fragmentation. This house consolidates the essence of reductiveness characteristic of my parents' house. It separates itself from the body of our work and represents a critical moment in my development. It possesses a primariness that is intuitive, unrepetitive, and uncontaminated. There is an elemental aspect to this house—a pure sense of spatial and volumetric manipulation and intensity—that is reassuring. The materiality, the spatial clarity, the selection of every object and every piece of art confirms its essentialness.

View from south   *Detail of southeast facade from service court*

354   *Detail of southeast facade from service court*

356   *Detail of southwest facade from entry court*

Gallery to entry hall

Detail of entry hall stair

mr als eine Milliarde Galaxien

Entry hall, gallery, and dining from stair

Dining gallery from stair   *Dining gallery from library*   *361*

Living from study balcony   *Study balcony*

View of upper roof garden to Alps

Detail of southeast facade   **369**

Master bath

San Onofre Residence

The San Onofre residence is located in a quiet residential neighborhood at the beginning of the Pacific Palisades Canyon. When we first started this project, I drove up to a cul-de-sac and was presented with an incredible view on a site that was basically at the edge of a palisade. I stood there and realized that this site existed at the intersection of two evocative view extensions: the Pacific Palisades Canyon to the west, and the ocean horizon, beyond Santa Monica, to the south. The contrast between these two landscapes was catalytic. On the plane that afternoon, I drew the diagram of the house—the idea that this would be a binuclear parti seemed irrefutable—a "Canyon House" containing the "non-public" spaces, and a "pavilion" that overviewed the ocean and contained the primary living spaces. The parti never changed.

The canyon house was designed as a building in the ground, anchoring and stabilizing the pavilion, an object on the ground. Separate, unique, and contrapuntal in its organization and its materiality, the pavilion, with its curved limestone wall, could be read as a found object, an archaeological fragment, transforming the experience of the landscape as one moves through it from the ordered programmatic distribution of the canyon house.

The canyon house is embedded in the ground and is organized vertically and bilaterally. Contained in the light-filled perimeter that overviews the canyon are the exercise room on the ground level, the children's bedrooms on the entry level, and an office/conference suite on the upper level. In the core, a screening room and a library occupy the ground level, storage and service areas are behind the garage on the entry level and, on the upper level, the master dressing room and bath, opposite the offices, are on axis with the bridge that connects to the pavilion.

The core of the pavilion, housing the master bedroom on the upper level and the kitchen on the entry level, floats within the limestone perimeter wall. It is an object

in a frame, a fragment of the canyon building that has been pulled through, forming the complex volumetric element that separates the double-height living and dining spaces. The breakfast room penetrates the screen of the brise soleil on the south glazed facade, and creates an outdoor terrace extension off the master bedroom above. At ground level, the entertainment room, the base of the core element, mediates the stone wall as an object in the frame which, in turn, defines a covered terrace that opens to the southern lawn and accesses the swimming pool and spa facing the canyon.

In addition to the two house structures, there is a third element—the site building. Creating the site—extending the two horizontal planes at different levels—involved constructing massive retaining walls (with caissons extending sixty-five feet to bed rock) and provided a unique opportunity for site integration and building organization. If one removed the house from the land, the retaining walls would be a formally resolved composition, as well as a transformed ruin.

The site structuring and the canyon house are both informed by the Zumikon residence, where the site structure and building are simultaneous. Zumikon is read as a series of erosions that result in a coherent whole, where the canyon house and the pavilion are separate, distinct, primary objects forming a collaged trilogy with the landscape walls.

When one passes through the gate at the end of the cul-de-sac, to the grass courtyard where cars are parked under the trees, a fragment of the stone wall is revealed, as is the east facade of the canyon house. The sequential unfolding of the site begins upon entering the house through the link element. Whether one enters on the main level or on the lower ground level, views of the canyon through the stair, and of the ocean through the pavilion, are immediately revealed. At that moment, the integration of the site is revealed, and the intersection of the stair and the bridge reconciles the vertical and horizontal connection of the two elements.

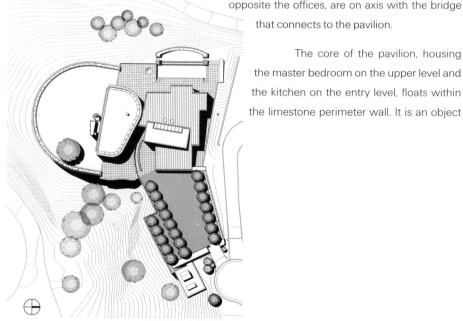

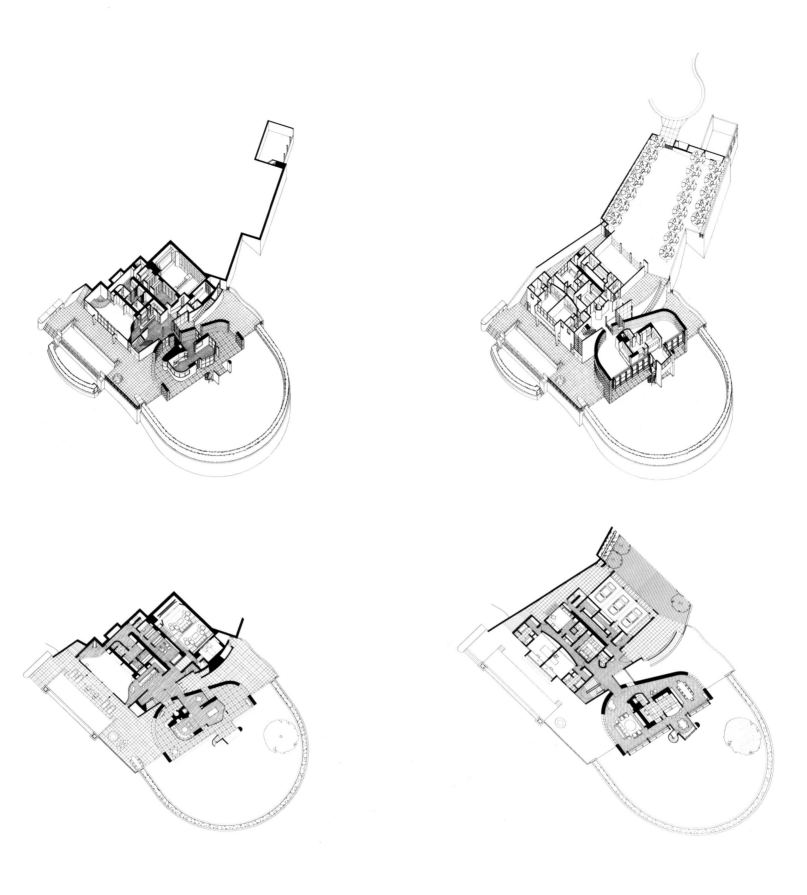

Ground, main, and upper level plans and axonometrics; overall axonometric

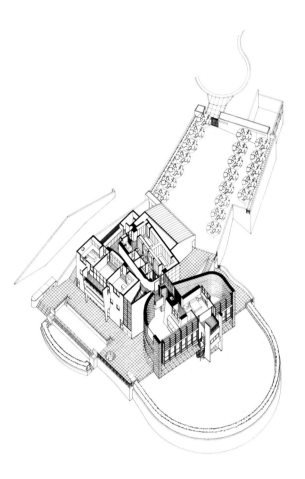

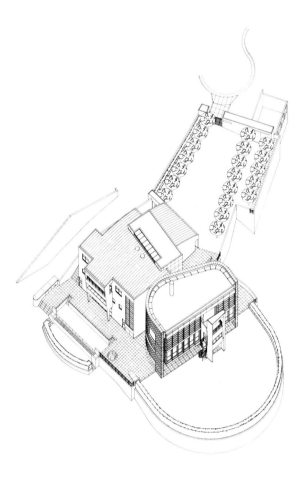

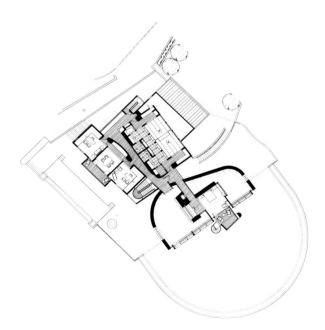

The link is the volumetric lock. On a purely intellectual level, resolving that formal issue was incredibly rewarding and emancipating—to discover a way to create a binuclear composition and resolve the parti, which we were taught at Yale could never be formally resolved. To enter through the link and have it serve as the connector, rather than the separator, was a breakthrough. Up until this house, we had always looked at composites, at making a holistic and unified series of partis. Even when, as in the Oceanfront, Taft, or Zumikon residences, we pulled the program apart and created separate outdoor and indoor spaces, the fabric of the buildings were all consistent. Here the elements are different formally and materially, while coexisting and interacting with, and enriching each other. The dynamics of the interlock between the two, the passage between the two, sensing the thickness of the stone wall, the different textures, and the different materialities, make this house a cubist collage that consolidates the spirit of and articulates the possibilities of fragmentation, collage, and discrepancy. The house becomes both a summary of thirty years of investigation and a breakthrough, freeing me to look both back and forward, to clarify and to reconcile. Designing this house showed me that it is possible to create pieces, to create fragments that are different from each other, and combine them to create a richer composition.

Southeast corner from bottom of bluff

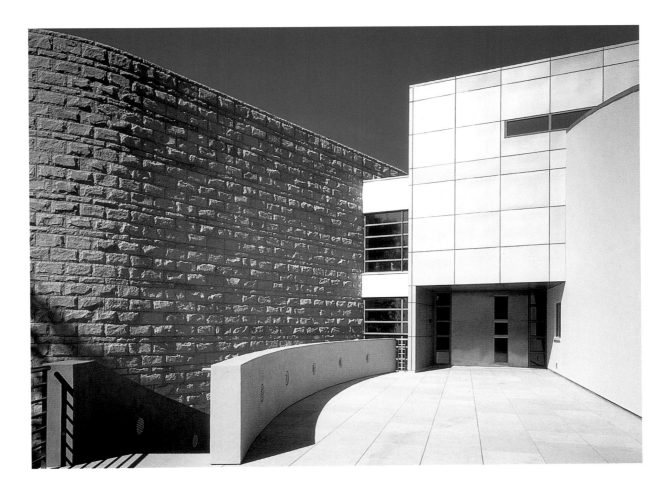

East facade from auto court

Main-level entry terrace from southeast

Ground-level entry terrace   Detail of exterior stair connecting upper- and lower-level entry terraces   *Detail from lawn terrace*   **381**

Stair gallery from entry   *Stair gallery from living*   *Detail of entry gallery from living*   383

Living   *Living from upper-level balcony   Living and upper-level balcony and bridge*

Master bedroom from dining   *Detail of upper-level bridge and skylight*   *Bridge and skylight from dining*   *Living from breakfast*   **387**

Master bath

Detail of south facade

389

Upper-level gallery

Upper-level stair landing   *Stair and canyon from upper-level stair landing*

Stair and bar from ground-level entry gallery

Ground-level entry gallery

Ground-level covered terrace

Detail from southwest   West facade and Santa Monica from pool terrace   South facade from lawn terrace (overleaf)

Hilltop Residence

The Hilltop residence is the largest house we have built to date. It is located on a previously undeveloped, wooded, eighty-five-acre site with views of the lakes, downtown Austin, and the University of Texas. It is programmatically unique in that it consolidates two distinct requirements in a single building—a "family house" program and an independent "entertainment" program, with extensive on-site parking to accommodate large family gatherings and business functions. The resolution of these two programs establishes the scale of the building and was critical in generating the parti.

The building is organized around a horizontal spine, with the "family house" and the "entertainment house" designed as complex figural objects integrated into the landscape and anchoring the two ends. The strategy refers back to the Taft house, where the spine concept was incubated, and the Opel house, in which a linear series of pavilions was organized along a spine. Diagrammatically, this is a more elaborated and complex resolution of the parti—the spine, as well as being the primary circulation element, is programmatically dense and is the site definer.

The automatic response to the site would have been to place the building on the top of the hill. Instead, this house, like the San Onofre and Gimelstob residences, is both in and on the land. With the San Onofre and Gimelstob houses, we responded to a found condition; here we created the grade change by building a plateau on the eastern portion of the site. The spine becomes a thick retaining wall, mediating between the existing , lower-grade entry level and the raised, private view level of the site. The house and the topography are integrated, simultaneously transforming the perception of the landscape and the house.

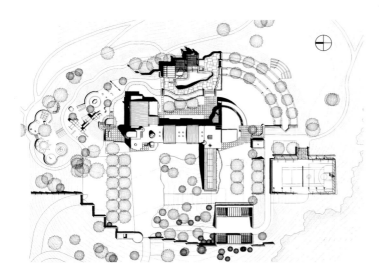

View east from entry gates

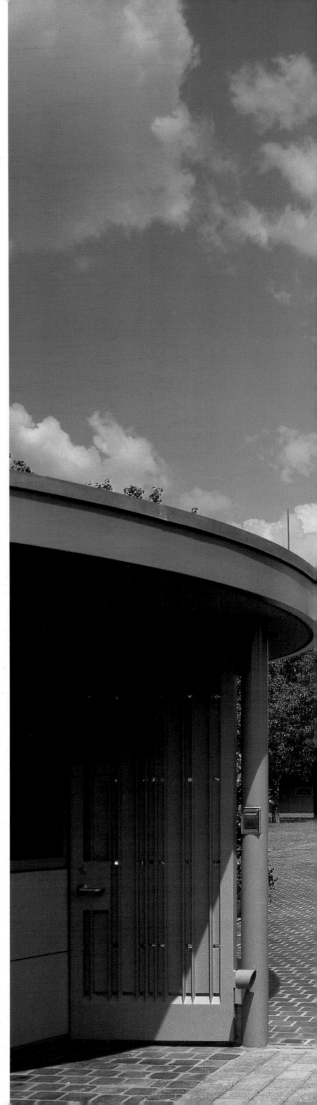

402   *Model shot from northwest; model shot from southwest*

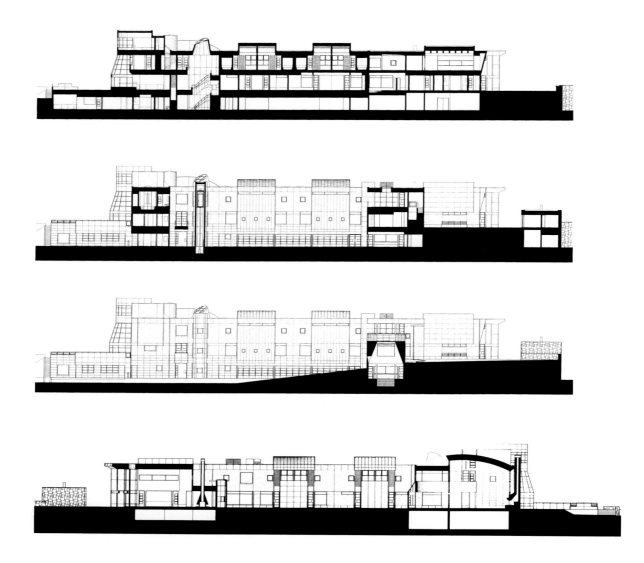

The arrival sequence is a mile-long drive culminating in a gated auto court fronting the three-story entry facade of the "family house," located at the north end of the spine. It is modulated by the entry, which accesses the main living level and a series of outdoor terraces by way of a skylit, elliptical grand staircase, as well as by the elevator element, and the double-height glazed breakfast room that extends onto an outdoor dining terrace overviewing the lake beyond. The double-height living room is extended by a screened sitting porch opening to the terraces and the pool pavilions. The spa, exercise room, and children's playroom are integrated into the spine and open onto the same terraces.

The double-height "entertainment pavilion," a segmented curve located at the south end of the spine, is accessed by way of a landscaped ramp to the upper-level courtyard. It is modulated by a stainless steel S-curved library and extended by a sweep of glazed doors opening onto a series of landscaped, stepped terraces that overview downtown Austin. The upper terrace can be covered by a tent structure designed to integrate the indoor and outdoor entertainment spaces.

The natatorium, forming the south wall of the entry court, with its curved, canted, skylit roof, is the third primary object on the spine. It mediates the site ramp and creates a cross-axial boundary between the private and the entertainment zones of the house.

The pairing of indoor and outdoor spaces continues around the perimeter of the house in a series of smaller pavilions that modulate the primary objects. In each, the sectional and volumetric interlocks that have been part of the "house

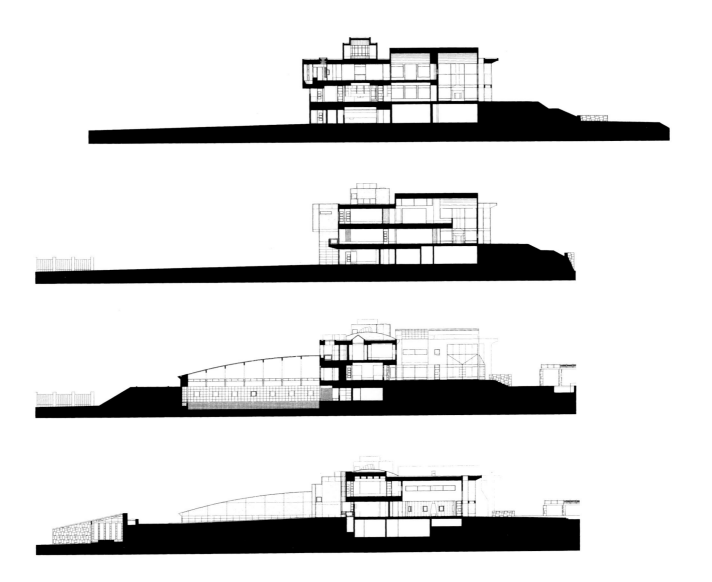

investigations" over the years have been refined and consolidated into a series of variations that articulate and modulate the building. The articulation, revelation, and sectional animation of these parts create a series of volumes that, in their own right, could be separate houses.

Like San Onofre, the composition is complex, fragmented, and collage assembled, accommodating differences and variations within the program and the site. The house is a series of experiences; it is read and understood sequentially rather than simultaneously. Forms are rendered as objects within an overall framework, and the fragmentation reinforces the composite as well as layered strategies. The material palette has been extended to further articulate volumetric and planar hierarchies. The base, engaging the grade, is granite; the primary walls are stucco, counterpointed by stainless steel panels and zinc standing-seam roofs and object

elements. The interior materials are maple, cherry, limestone, and slate floors; pearwood cabinets, doors, and bases; and integral plaster walls and ceilings.

Though this house and San Onofre were designed at the same time, they are very different. Each, in its own way, edits, consolidates, and extends the discoveries of thirty years. If there is anything that I have learned from these houses, it is that even with greater asymmetrical complexity and more spatial and volumetric variation, there is still a sense of calm. I remember Louis Kahn saying that the aspiration of his buildings, aside from making a place, was to make a "quiet" space. In each of these houses, we have accomplished that goal. There is a stillness that allows the natural and the man-made to coexist in a way that is enriching, dynamic, and speculative, while engaging both the present and the future.

Detail of west facade from upper-ground-level courtyard   *Detail of south facade from upper-ground-level terrace*

Detail from southwest   *North view from lower ground level*   *Tennis/play court*   *Tennis/play court*

Detail of entertainment pavilion   *Entertainment pavilion from stepped terrace*   *View of south facade from below stepped landscape terrace*   **415**

Pool terrace and pavilion from balcony

Detail of pool terrace pavilion

Pool terrace pavilion from lower level

Entertainment pavilion with tent and library from upper-ground-level terrace (previous pages)   *Detail of entertainment pavilion*   *Detail of library and arcade*

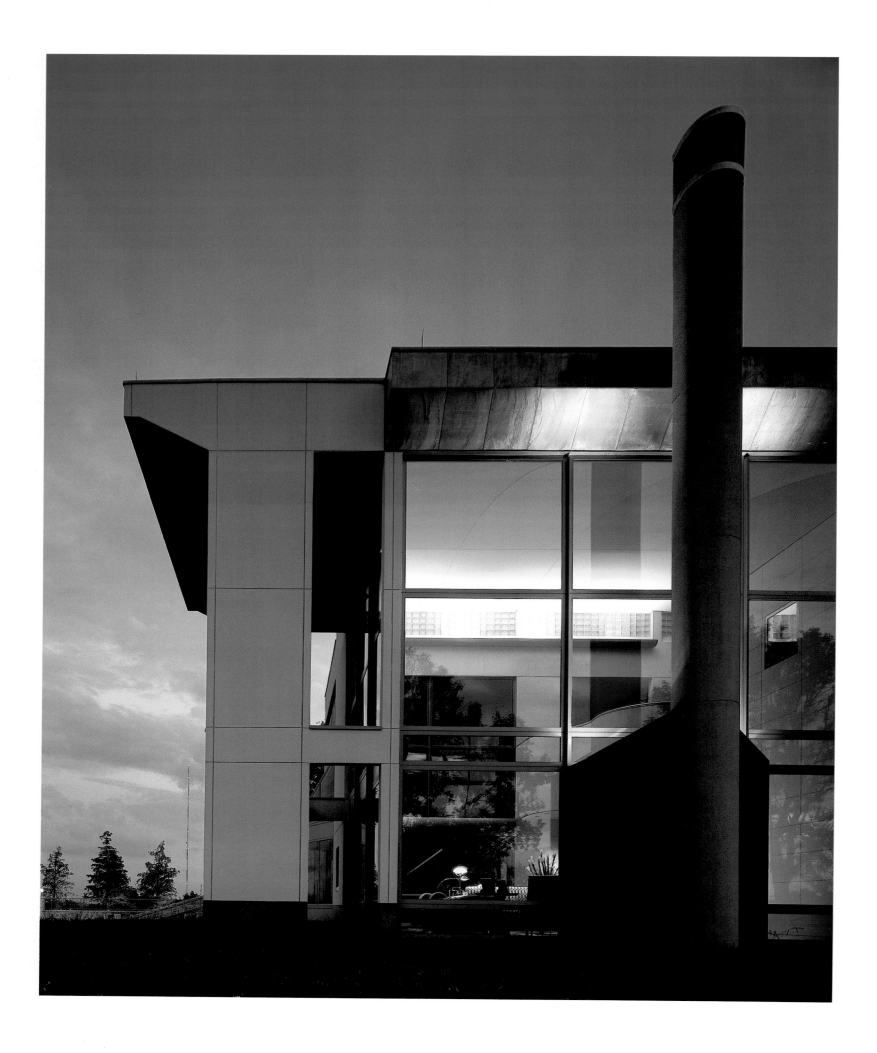

Detail of northwest corner

Detail of stair and elevator, second level

Gallery from second-level stair landing

Screened porch to terrace

Breakfast room **449**

Spiral stair

Lap pool

Lap pool to playroom balcony   *Lap pool from playroom*

Entertainment room (previous pages)   *Entertainment room*   *Game room/library*

Sitting/library   Entry gallery from sitting   *Detail of stair*

Bedroom gallery

Conference room/screening room

Conference room/screening room

Guest bedroom

Photography Credits

Assassi Productions

Oceanfront Residence
Photographs on pp. 324–25, 328–47
San Onofre Residence
All photographs except pp. 382, 383 (bottom left), 393 (bottom)

Otto Baitz

Benenson Residence
All photographs

Richard Bryant/Arcaid

Garey Residence
All photographs
Spielberg Residence
All photographs except pp. 262–63
Opel Residence
All photographs
Zumikon Residence
All photographs except pp. 367, 369 (bottom)

Anita Calero

San Onofre Residence
Photograph on pp. 382, 383 (bottom left), 393 (bottom)

David Franzen

Cohn Residence
All photographs

Yukio Futagawa

Sedecca Residence
Photograph on pp. 58–59
Tolan Residence
Photographs on pp. 91 (bottom), 92–93, 94–95

David Hirsch

Gwathmey Residence
Photographs on pp. 12–13, 16–17, 19 20, 21–35, 36–37
Tolan Residence
Photographs on pp. 88–89

Mancia/Bodmer

Zumikon Residence
Photographs on pp. 367, 369 (bottom)

Bill Maris

Gwathmey Residence
Photograph on pp. 38–39
Straus Residence
All photographs
Sedecca Residence
All photographs except pp. 58–59
Goldberg Residence
All photographs
Cooper Residence
All photographs
Tolan Residence
Photographs on pp. 84–85, 91 (top), 93–94

Norman McGrath

Gwathmey Residence
Photographs on pp. 18, 36 (top)
Haupt Residence
All photographs
Weitz Residence
All photographs
de Menil Residence
All photographs except pp. 219, 223 (top), 227 (bottom)
Viereck Residence
All photographs
Spielberg Residence
Photograph on pp. 262–63
Gimelstob Residence
All photographs

Richard Payne

Taft Residence
All photographs
Hilltop Residence
All photographs

Roberto Schezen

Gwathmey Residence
Photograph on pp. 36 (bottom)
de Menil Residence
Photographs on pp. 219, 223 (top), 227 (bottom)

Ezra Stoller/Esto

Gwathmey Residence
Photograph on pp. 2–4, 6 (bottom)
Cogan Residence
All photographs